PRAISE FOR

Cante Bardo: A Song Between Lives

"This novel is a masterpiece. *Cante Bardo* is a classic whose plot enchants the reader with a style that is poetic in its execution."

– Carole Muir, *ForeWord Reviews*

"Lisa Smartt's beautifully written *Cante Bardo* takes readers on a magical journey as she shares with them the ineffable beauty and sheer power that is at the heart of both flamenco and the near-death experience."

– Dr. Raymond Moody, author of *Life After Life*

"Whether you read Lisa Smartt's *Cante Bardo* as a true account of an Angel of Death seeking forgiveness for his past life, or as a daring novel about reincarnation, Spanish gypsies, flamenco and modern-day passion, you will find yourself entranced. The sheer power of Smartt's writing carries us along with her

characters through tumultuous events and those small shifts in
the human heart that are equally powerful in determining
destinies."

— Margot Silk Forrest, author of *A Short Course in Kindness*

"Smartt writes this story as if the rhythms were born
into her blood, and the language and hardships of the
people were part of her bones... bringing us into a world
few of us have visited. *Cante Bardo* is a passionate,
gutsy and mystical triumph. Bravo!"

— Carolyn North, author of *The Experience of a Lifetime*

"Lisa Smartt offers a compelling poetic tale of the soul's
journey to wholeness across centuries and cultures...
Cante Bardo is filled with images of the radiant and
mysterious."

— J. Ruth Gendler, author of *The Book of Qualities*

CANTE BARDO:

A Song Between Lives

Lisa Smartt

ISBN-13: 978-1721902064

ISBN-10: 1721902066

www.theuniversityofheaven.com

Dedicated to my husband John Smartt
whose love has brought me home
and Raymond Moody
whose generous heart guided me through
the words between the worlds.

TABLE OF CONTENTS

1. ASSASSIN   11

2. THE MAGICIAN'S ASSISTANT   27

3. THE FLOWERING VEIL   43

4. THE SEANCE   61

5. HOME FOR THE POOR   73

6. HANDS   87

7. ESCAPE ARTIST   107

8. ANGELICA   119

9. CANTAOR   131

10. ZAPOTEANDO   147

11. SAND   161

12. THE LOCKET   177

13. ALTEA   199

14. SACRED MOUNTAIN   219

AFTERWORD   237

I did not begin when I was born, nor when I was conceived.
I have been growing, developing,
through incalculable myriads of millenniums.
All my previous selves have their voices,
echoes, promptings in me.
Oh, incalculable times again shall I be born.

Jack London

1.

ASSASSIN

Ya viene el Cristo Moreno

El Señor de los gitanos

El más grande y el más gueno.

Apretaitas las manos

Pobre Jesús Nazareno.

Here comes the dark-skinned Christ

Lord of the gypsies

With hands bound

Poor Jesus of Nazareth.

I go because I must.

I slip into the room and watch, but then I must take action. The body is no longer pink. There is the queasy gray that I know all too well, the blue-slate of impending death. The mother rocks back and forth with the exhale of her tears. She will not let him go easily. He is the fruit of her womb, the little blueberry plucked out.

"There is no hope here," I whisper. Mother's hands move in circles on the infant's forehead. Soon I will descend.

"Baby, I wish you did not have to..." I whisper, but my sorrows will not be answered.

Instead I pick up one of heaven's violins and embrace it. My cheek rests against the hard bone of wood, against the howling hardness of its music. I have come to take this child back home. I am the thief of breath, the keeper of dreams. I am Carlos, Angel of Death, assigned by God to take life.

The gust of my hands sucks away the last wheeze. The convulsing begins. I hate the terrible crying. "I know, I know. It is hard to leave," I say, "but you know it's time." The baby's golden soul follows me. We leave behind the nursery with its teddy bears and rocking chair, and a shadow casts a veil over the room of toys and blankets.

Flowers bend with the weight of his absence. A rose petal fades, curls at the edges.

And then all is still.

The soul travels into the night where we dead go to meet our Maker. I leave the young corpse at the foot of Saint Michael. He crouches down to touch the infant, nodding as if he is saying, "You have done your job well, Carlos." The journey between Earth and heaven is a silent one. I do my work quickly, as I must, and go back to the executioner's quarters. Tonight I am heavier with sadness than usual. These are the words of a gypsy singer, a flamenco cantaor, whose song fails him, whose tired throat no longer sings. The violin does the work of my voice, swiftly slicing at the air, swiftly wishing for a dancer to give its song meaning.

I think of Angelica, lost in spins, her hair wild and dark. I wish she were here with me and we were sharing red wine again in the cafés, sharing the dances of Cádiz. But that was then. And now not only distances but time separates us. Somewhere in heaven, she dances still or perhaps is back on Earth in some village where the sailors come with their quarters to watch her. She must be a dancer in her new life as well, for that was all she was—it seemed all she ever could be. She was a temple for muses, a shrine for the unholy to worship. Inspiration found itself in her toes, in the swift stabs of flamenco's feet, of duende inhabiting flesh. Do you know duende? The stirring of soul as it moves through the veins? Duende is the spirit, the force without face, which brings poets to the pen and dancers to the floor. Some might call it muse or inspiration, but it has its darkness, like the passion of a kiss that is stolen from another man's wife. Angelica housed duende; it slept and ate in the walls of her brown body.

Here in the executioner's quarters, there is a concrete floor, one bed, one chair and my old violin. I have a hook for my clothes and the old hat that has followed me from my days on Earth. My name is Carlos Peña. I was once a gypsy. Now I live in the sector of heaven that is home to the messengers of the dying. It is a very dark place. Jackals roam the barren landscape. There is never a sun or a moon here. This is where the evil ones do God's dirty work. We are like those slaves who do the laundry for the kings, our hands full of dirt and blood and the sweat of those in power. We are not commissioned to hell but to heaven's dark camp. We are the takers of life.

While you sleep in your lover's arms, cook dinner or watch the movies, I am waiting. I know when your time has come and breath must be coaxed from you. I go to old women in wheelchairs and children choking on peppermints. I say, "Come to me. Time to go home." And sometimes I take them into the light. There God meets them with an incredible brilliance. Some of you will enter light-filled tunnels. Others will pass through darkness. Some are easily led away, like blind dogs into starless nights. Others refuse me and struggle against these gypsy hands. There are attachments. Things you hate to leave: Aunt Sadie's sofa, your lover's sweet shoulder, the grandchildren. Even those who come willingly, leave behind a trail of tears. It's very hard work for a gypsy like me.

"You sing so sorrowfully," they told me when I first came to the Gates. "We have just the place for you, Carlos Peña." In the cold darkness of heaven's nights, I sing as I did in my last life—and the old violin has become my second voice. Each Death Angel has at least one instrument of death—one heralding call. Those who come with me will hear the frenzied wail of a gypsy's sad song or my fiddle slicing away at the silence. Have you heard me in your dreams? In your walks through the neighborhood? Have you heard my voice cut through the chorus of chanting cicadas... or heard the cat gut bow screeching against the strings?

In my mortal days, I had the misfortune of being a gypsy, born into a land that hated me, into a family that despised me. My early life was spent in pain. Later in violence. I became an assassin. Once by circumstance and twice by choice.

I was born in Jérez, Spain to Rosa, the mother I never met. I came through her narrow corridors like a thick pig. And I killed her. I tumbled out from the womb, sticky, hopelessly lost, into the frozen fingers of an aunt and grandmother who would never forgive my birth. I did not mean to kill her. My birth was, in itself, an act of violence.

I was a little hairless creature, like a lizard, grunting through the dark passages of her—and then the lights went out. First there was water, the rush of blood and then a narrow ridge, opening like the caves of Granada that I have scaled in the dark, rock and pebble beneath me and then nothing. That last breath, the push that killed her, the expanded womb, yielded a pair of little brown feet.

Mine.

The assassin was born.

It was my fate to take the lives of others. As I grew a little older, I killed two people as a childish prank—and as a young man, I took another life in a sacred reverie, a sick union with death. Two died by fire; the other by the snug blade of my knife. And it all started with the accidental assassin's first breath.

"A lifetime spent with death," God said. "You will be a good Death Angel. End their lives and lead them back to me." Yes, I am one of God's angels, but I do not inspire love, great symphonies or acts of selfless courage. I carry the sins of the Earth, so I am more like a mortal: wingless. The true angels have wings. The greater the spirit, the larger the span of them, like arcs of light that represents a soul's evolution. Archangels' wings tower in heaven, for their sprits have overcome mortal failings. But I am a death maker with the appearance of a human. I am unshaven and sad-eyed with no wings, just a body hollow of blood, tall and lanky with brown skin. It is the consequence of a life of so little love, of such great obsession with darkness.

It was a terrible mistake. I could have been a poet or even a minister of God, but a series of terrible realities led me to this: to my anger, my fanatic sprees, to decades of service as a Death Angel. From one world to another, I am God's midwife. Here every day, every hour, pulling the newly dead from their deathbeds as the cries of their loved ones fill the room. I tug, tug until the body surrenders. It's hard, hard work.

Before morning, I must go again through the layer of clouds into your world. I must find a young woman who will crash into the ocean. Her car full of flames, her body broken, like a book with no spine, its pages scattered into the sea. She will die while driving near the California Coast. She is beautiful, I am told, and her beauty has served her well but will mean nothing in the face of death. Her head will fly through the glass—young Jeannie Price—and her skull will shatter into pieces, vanity vanished.

The friends who await her will mourn as they all do. There will be the call to her mother and the siren which comes, itself a cante jondo—a deep song—from a red throat. "Jeannie is dead!" they will cry. And whoever she was—and whatever she was or wished to be—taken away.

Outside the jackals fight among themselves. I have learned to walk past them without fear. They have attacked me with their teeth. And of course I survive. For everything in heaven is ethereal, made of spirit not matter. In heaven we face what on Earth had no face. The jackals are the roaming dark of my own thoughts. Their yapping jaws remind me of the hell I have created by my own bad deeds. Every day they howl and pace. I have offered them my meatless arm, have defended myself with my fiddle. Sometimes they dig into me, and I howl back with the memory of pain. It is an afterlife full of suffering. Tonight, like every night, I must go again and kill, out the door into the coldness of the death camp down into Earth.

I am led to her as she drives through the rolling seaside hills. The van is surrounded in a blue light that is visible only to me; it is the mark of death, the color of stolen life. I slip through the fog and approach. On the van is a photograph: A dark-eyed woman with a full head of black hair, smiles as she points a wand to a rabbit in a hat. I pause to look again. Wands?

Rabbits? There are words. I do not read very well—in any language—but I recognize m-a-g-i-c, like the Spanish mágico. Magic? I slip through the window into the car's seat to see the same girl, but she's not frozen into a photograph. She whistles while she taps her feet, very much alive. Magician? Can she escape chains and make things appear and disappear?

I remember hearing of men who could swallow needles and gulp large gusts of fire. Magicians threw themselves into the bottom of the sea locked and chained and would emerge again free men. Back in my day, I heard stories but I never saw these great magicians.

I look at her and feel a tug of warmth. Is she a magic girl? I sit beside her. She is young. How sad to die now! In her face, I see the strong frailty of girls I have known, like the pouting beauty, Angelica, or Patia, my wise sister. Yes, magic. There is heat in my chest where my heart once was. Maybe I have known Jeannie before in another life, another time. Girl who does tricks: Were you once Patia? The girl puckers her lips and then her eyes widen as if they catch sight of me, but none of it is conscious. Death is often seen but the mind cannot make sense of it. I know she senses me. I know it, so I grin for her, wishing I could take her cheeks into my hands and kiss them.

Her presence sings to me with the power of Spanish soil, pulls me towards her and away from the thin railing that will splinter, sending her into the ocean. It is time to push her into the sea, but instead I stare dumbly, stretching comfortably in the car's seat. In my day, it would have taken hours to cross these roads by foot or even horseback, but now we are fast as wind with the blur of blue sea beside us.

Then I hear bells.

I forget time, but I know I must take her. I must do it now.

Once they were merely targets, but I have been flirting with life again. I see beauty in the flowers, rocks and trees again— and even in my charges. My instinct to kill is completely dulled. I am tired of my work, like a blacksmith who has lost his desire for metal and fire. No, I am no longer thinking of death but of dancing and red wine. I am imagining fresh bread on a wooden table and the lovely sound of women laughing. I imagine dancing with the girl in Cádiz. Would she have been moved by my cantes?

She looks again at me, and I wish there were no veil between us. I say to her, "Beautiful evening for a dance. Do you dance?" I feel God's impatient tug from above.

What if I let her go? What if this time I walk away from death?

I ask myself these questions, but I know I have no choice. I must do the work of a Death Angel, for that it all I have earned for myself in the course of my days, my past life.

I throw the car into the railing and then pull it to the other side slamming the walls of granite. The car slides across the highway, but I cannot pull the wheels over into the sea.

Carlos Peña will not take that final step towards death. The metal screams as it scrapes against the railing. The car slows to a stop, its doors crushed. The car teeters, daring the sea below.

But I cannot kill her.

"I can't. I can't," I cry, looking up at God and then down at the girl's dazed face. I glance at her frightened eyes. Her hands struggle to her face as a shiver passes through her body. She looks around and then at me as if she hears my cries. "I can't, God. I can't take the girl."

I know I must send her and the car into the rocks and waves below but cannot.

I see the faded pink of aura around her—the aura of life. I stare at her in stunned silence, for I am paralyzed and can do nothing more. She looks at me, her mouth open like a child's, and then she curls and uncurls her hands stiffly as if they were not her own. I stand near her, my fingertips hungering to feel her, but a Death Angel can only bring the dead home, cannot touch his charge, not with the healing touch of love.

I move above her, still with the heart torn towards life. As I slip slowly away, toward the heavens, I hear wheels on the misty concrete below. A green car comes around the corner and screeches to a stop. "Are you okay?" I hear the driver cry, his hands pulling on the handle on the dented frame.

"Who are you?" she says tilting her head towards me, not him. I know she has seen me with my sad eyes and the face wet with tears. Often the dying, see those of us on the other side. You can see them reaching for us as the threshold door opens.

"I'll call an ambulance." The man is small and sturdy and lets out a groan as he widens the door. The girl I should have killed crawls out.

"I don't need an ambulance." Her jaw moves more slowly than words.

As I look below and move into the skies empty-handed, I wail out with the songs of an old gypsy. Too much death has broken this old angel's heart. The girl is bent in pain, and the man walks her to his car. From high above, I see the shapes moving, like small white insects against the tarred road below.

Ashamed, I return to the Pearly Gates without her. Saint Michael awaits. "Peter sent me to wait for you. He said you were bringing no dead home tonight."

He is standing there with a sky full of stars around him, his tall wings stretching high into the heavens. There is no anger or judgment in his voice, but I have trouble facing him. A gypsy man is a man of duty, and he must always keep his word—especially in heaven. I am a Death Angel who did not do his job. Saint Michael's wings form a heart around him. His caramel skin glitters beneath the starlit sky. My heart sinks. God will be disappointed in me. Saint Michael opens his arms, and I hesitate. "It's okay, Carlos. It's really okay." I collapse into his body weeping. I am afraid. There must be terrible punishment for betraying my responsibilities.

Saint Michael pulls away gently and looks into me. His eyes are black as well water. This is the first time we are alone together like this, and yet, he knows me as God knows the Earth. His kind face is framed by a small gray beard, wiry and close to his chin. His hand motions for me to follow.

"Come, Carlos." I limp behind him in sadness, across the meadows of heaven, in the dark of night, to the chamber of angels.

There was something about the girl," I say, swallowing words.

Saint Michael opens the door to the chamber. The beauty of the room stalls my steps. I have never been in any of the halls on this side of heaven where the muses and archangels live. All I know are the humble rooms of heaven's dark camp. The chamber has cathedral ceilings of gold and marble. One wall is built in limestone with a waterfall rushing down its side into a pool with rocks and lilies and birds. On another is a large golden cage with birds singing.

Saint Michael leads me to a velvet chair. "Sit, sit," he points.

"Will I have to leave heaven?" I ask. If God rejects me, there is little chance of redemption. I will be doomed to the Wheel of Hell, where the hopeless are, those who live in the heat of their evil, whose unwillingness dooms them to days of fever, to hours of futile tasks and slow evolution. Those who are sent to hell can wait decades, even centuries, before given the chance again to redeem their sins, come back to heaven and Earth, to grow.

"No, no. Do not worry. This is a good thing, Carlos. Really."

"A good thing?" I ask.

"I think so," he says, reaching for heaven's water, and offering a glass to me. "If you are truly ready."

"But I broke my promise to always bring back the dead . . . to never question God."

"You did you work," Saint Michael says.

"I did?"

"It happens sooner or later to Death Angels." He pauses. "But we can't assume it's time."

"Time? Time for what?"

"To leave behind your old identity, to become a source of inspiration, not death."

"Inspiration?"

"A muse, Carlos."

I am looking behind him at the singing birds; my heart warms with the promise of change. The birds jump from perch to perch, twig to twig. One moment we are one thing, and in the next we are another. I have learned this from being an Angel of Death— and a gypsy. Nothing is permanent. The angels who walk the heavens with large wings and bright smiles were once corpses whose cold hands were gray and lifeless. The man stiffened by death once ran to his bride with daisies. But I did not think Carlos Peña would ever be released from this purgatory.

"But we must be certain. That begins with looking back at your life, why you murdered before."

"Yes, I understand." If the appetite to kill is still there, I will kill again in my next life.

"Can you see, Carlos?" Saint Michael points. On the tallest wall is a large round circle, the shape and color of the full moon. "This is what we call the lunar table. It can be projected onto the walls or ceiling—or even into the palm of your hand." The light shifts from the wall into my hand, a white flickering dome. "The lunar table holds a record of each man and woman's past. Here are the images of your last life." I stare down at it. There in the center of my hand is a circle of light.

"Look into the table. The table of life, Carlos." The light jumps out of my palm and once again onto the large space before me. A picture appears on the wall: rolling hills and arbors without grapes, just clipped vines, weeks after the harvest.

"Jérez. I was born there," I say.

A crumbling house stands without windowpanes, open to the wind. I see bare feet walking slowly across pebbled soil. The brown toes pause at the door, and then step in. A woman's voice cries, "The baby. The baby is coming." It's as if seeing and feeling are the same sense. I turn to look up at Saint Michael, who watches with wonder as I do.

He rests his brown hand on my thigh. He has small, knotty fingers, like those of a laborer, and veins where blood once ran. They form ridges like a small blue mountain range "Humble beginnings," Saint Michael says, "in a beautiful land . . ."

I look up to see the bare vines and the empty trellises after harvest. I feel the damp October air, salted slightly by the sea— and I smell food cooking on the flame outside: old scraps of meat softened with garlic and tomatoes. A breeze sweeps over the cracked floor, past the faces of my aunt and grandmother, to the clenched fist of a woman. It is my mother. The year is 1884. I, Carlos Peña, am about to be born.

2.
THE MAGICIAN'S ASSISTANT

Qué desgracia terelo
Mare en el andar
Como los pasos que
P'alante daba
Se me van atrás

What misfortune strikes me, mother,
Whenever I go about.
The steps
Meant to bear me forward
Carry me back.

The land where I am born was once a sea. I imagine this sea when I am young as I look out at the open horizon. When I am sick or too hot, I can see the earth tip to one side or another as if the waves still swell beneath the chalk-white earth, where now there is a tide of ripe vines with plump green and red grapes, uvas. Uvas, uvas, the pearls of our land, scar our fingers and bring bread to the table. The grapes are cut and gathered by gypsies like me. Deep within the dim wine cellars, *las bodegas*, the golden grapes age into sherry. The song says, "The flower thrives in darkness." The flower is the veil of yeast that protects the sherry from the air and flourishes in the silent cellars of Jérez. The high windows keep the sun from the barrels, and a curtain of dry grass invites air but not the light.

But not the light.

And I am curled in the silent dark of my mother, hanging in the wineblood of her, in that world when a soul is what it is, merely itself, without a name, a face, just suspended in the moon of her, in that twilight before birth, in a safe small place.

And I am protected by the thin sheath of skin, like the flowering veil, that keeps me from the world outside. I sink into the wonderful heat of her and feel the presence of God— for in here, mother and God are one. And then the rush, the breaking of the dam. Her womb insists. I must leave. I feel the quickening of a body ready to spit out its child, but I am not ready. I want to stay here with mother, and the happy sounds. *Don't make me go yet*, I want to cry, but it all happens so fast. I am battling bones and fluid, like rocks and current, swept into the red rapids—*help me*. I know it is too quick, and something is wrong. I am caught—as it was when the Earth was born, an explosion so intense and gaseous—full of poisons as well as life—and then, a deafening heartbeat. And everything slows. I am fighting my way against the gravity, my head aimed towards light. But her body is limp. I am surrounded by the tomb of her.

I know immediately that death has me, and I am sure I will die too. Her body traps me. It is heavy and full of water, and then I am pulled out. There are screams and the cries, "Ay, María!" I see candles, a blur of yellow, and hear the loud wail. My mother, Rosa, is dead.

Rosa looks nothing like me. Her face is plump, round, like a child's, and her long hair is completely gypsy, black and straight, weighed down by the sweat of labor and death. She lies there, her hands stretched out at her sides, her fingers curled. She rests in her bed, in a coffin of our blood, in the mix of birth. The statue of the Virgin stands at the foot of her bed, the cold granite hands in prayer for me. I come out, like that, through the walls of death, through the pink tomb of mother, her wet shores as blue as my sleep.

The mother I never knew left a canyon in my heart. The face of my maternal grandmother points to the shivering newborn, me. "He is not one of us. Put him in the other room, away," she says to my sister Flavia.

My grandmother is Flora, but she is no flower. The stem of her spine is stiff and cruel, like a stick without petals. She is also known as La Cicatriz, the scar, for the woman has a long old wound from her eye to her chin. She bends to her knees at the corpse of her daughter, puts her hands in prayer.

"Come, come," she says to the man who stands near her. "Pray with me." She then whispers, so the others will not hear, "Is she forgiven for betraying you?"

"Is that my father?" I ask Saint Michael in a whisper. The man is like me covered in skin as dark as a raisin.

"Yes," Saint Michael says. "It's Eduardo . . ."

"He is my real father?"

"Yes, yes . . . shhh," Saint Michael says. In the dark, I see the outline of his finger pressed against his lips. "Shhh . . ."

My eyes stare into the image of my father as he crouches onto the floor near his wife, my mother. He looks at the corpse before him surrounded in the amber of candlelight. He leans into her ear, looks as if he is biting it, for his jaw is clenched and his eyes squint in rage. His face and hair is dark; his nose is long and sharp. He hisses into her neck and then quietly steps away.

It's the hiss of a man deceived, for what he hears in my cries is the breath of a payo, a Spaniard. I am not gypsy, he believes, but made of a payo's blood, made of the vinegar of Spaniard's love, of bitter kisses that fell onto his wife's betraying lips.

"Bastard," he whispers.

I am left alone covered in blood and wrapped in one old rag. My eight-year-old sister, Patia, walks in, crouches down to look at me.

My grandmother cries, "Come here, come here girl, now." But she does not listen. "Poor baby," Patia says. She puts her pinky into my mouth, so I can suck, and then strokes me. Her little hand rubs away the blood. "They didn't even clean you."

With the corner of her shirt, she shines my head, behind my ears. As she touches me, it is as if all the cells in my body recognize that we are made of the same substance, and it calms me. The others will descend upon me with hatred, but Patia and I are connected by soul. She can read my eyes; she knows that in the dark of my pupil is the desire for light. She sees the music in me before there is music. The others will envy her for her sharp vision. She sees things others do not. When she is older, she will tell fortunes.

Maybe she does not understand that her mother, our mother, lies dead in the other room, but she comes to me, gravitates to my eyes as if we were pulled together. She strokes my head, bald and wrinkled. My whole life I cannot recover from those hours after my birth. The resonance of those moments do not end; the vibrating, terrified soul never catches its breath. I am breathless always. Patia hums, just as she does when I am a man and cannot find my way.

"A dear girl," says Saint Michael. The room now is completely black, so I cannot see him but only hear his voice rise from his faint silhouette.

"Yes," I say, swallowing with sadness, "she was." The light of the lunar table fills the room. On the screen Patia sings, "No cradle for the baby. He will sleep right here. No cradle for the baby."

Patia sings until I slip into my first sleep. Her black hair swirls around her face. Her arms, belly, legs engulf me. Her heart is small, not quite a drum, but a small tambourine. In the dark of night, when I am hungry, she gets milk from the mama goat. When I cannot drink from the cup, she puts the white nectar into her mouth and feeds it to me through her kisses.

Two mornings after my mother is buried, my father Eduardo leaves with a diligencia, a caravan of rented horses, to Granada.

When Flora finds his empty chair and the wooden box without money, she screams, "Dios mío! He's left! Eduardo has left!" She runs to wake her husband and her sister, Ana. "Everything is gone," she cries out. "All this work lost for the sins of her." She stares out at the rows of bare vines and then runs to my sleeping sister.

"Get Patia away from the boy," she tells Flavia. Flora's scar breathes with rage. "He is bad luck." Flavia pulls Patia by her thin arms across the floor. Her eyes grow big in fear and her body startles.

La Cicatriz leans into her face. "Do as I say. Go start the fire and stay away from the baby." Patia rushes into the chilly air.

Flavia, who is twelve, comes into the room. "Where is daddy? Where did he go?"

Grandfather says with a mouth old from sun and living in the wind, "He probably went home to his people in Granada."

"Is it far?" Sara, who is only six, trails in after Flavia.

"Far, very far." Grandfather clears his throat. His eyes fill with sadness.

"It's him," my grandmother says, pointing to my little body, almost blue from cold. "He did it. Your father did not like the boy, so he left, left us alone here."

"Him? The baby?" Flavia says.

"Baby? No, he's a demon. He killed your mother and made your daddy leave," Flora says.

Patia walks in with hands dirtied from soot, from the makings of fire.

"Daddy's gone," Flavia points, "because of him."

"Daddy's gone?" Patia asks. I lie there, a crying baby on the cold stone floor.

I search Saint Michael's gaze in the dark but cannot find it. "Only a few days after my birth and it was already too late..." A pain spreads throughout my body, a grief so powerful and without words. It's as if the suffering of that small baby completely fills me. The pain begins at my navel where the string was cut that tied me to my dead mother.

"You had little chance, it's true. It's a miracle they didn't kill you," Saint Michael speaks to me in the dark. I become afraid without light.

"My guts hurt," I say.

"That's the pain of the unloved boy—pain that became anger. Pain that became the music of El Huérfano...The

Orphan..."

Saint Michael's wings press into the chair. "One child's pain leads to another's."

"What?"

"The Wheel of Karma. Those who get hurt often hurt others... but not the great ones. They go on to heal and inspire."

"Not me," I hang my head in shame. "I just didn't know how to..."

"I know," Saint Michael almost sings now, repeating the chorus. " One child's pain leads to another...and...another..."

As he sings, the room becomes completely dark, and I am floating in space, flying as I usually do to bring back the dead, but there are no corpses waiting for me, no thread of light that leads me to my charges, just my body spiraling down into Earth, spiraling into the dense and gravity-filled world.

I land in a darkened room. As my eyes adjust, I can see that it is a theatre.

"Cut the spot." Two silhouettes stand there. One is a tall woman, the other small and round.

The tall girl looks out into the rows of empty chairs. "How long do we have?" It's the girl. The magician.

"Ten minutes." The short, round girl has a head full of wild curls.

"Okay, good...Can I get some light here?"

Jeannie Price, the girl I could not kill, steps onto the

stage. She wears a sparkling red dress, short to the edges of her thighs.

"I need a man to put this Jeannie in...a bottle..." she says, walking to the edge of the stage where a large glass bottle stands—just a little bigger than she is.

"We'll bring him in stage right. . . Sandra, are you listening?"

"Yeah." The girl holds a clipboard and steps into the light of the stage. Her curls are golden, and she looks like a little angel. "Come on in," she calls out to the back of the room. When the doors open, a man of thirty walks in. He is small and muscular and strolls down the aisle with the authority of the privileged.

Jeannie looks up as he walks towards her, "You look so familiar," then pausing. "But I can't place you."

"Greg," he heads for the stage. "Greg Taylor... I..."

"Oh my goodness." She climbs down the stairs and reaches her hand out to him in recognition. "Greg... Great to see you."

"Sandra this is the guy I was telling you about... from the accident..."

"Wow... of all the crazy things..."

"I came to try out for magician's assistant," he says.

"Magician's assistant--eh?"

"I saw the ad in the paper. Just thought I would give it a try. Had hoped you would remember me."

"Ever done anything like this? Get onto the stage with me," Jeannie motions to the large bottle. "You're sweet on the eyes... just a little on the short side. Let me see you over there. Stage left, over there." Jeannie steps back to look. "How did you find me?" she asks coming close to him.

"Saw the ad in *The Herald*. You're a little hard to miss..."

"Hmm...could you take your shirt off?"

"My shirt... sure..."

"So now that you've found me. . .tell me what you know about magic."

Greg Taylor looks out into the theatre. His stare lands on me. Does he see Carlos Peña? "Magic... well ... my interest started in high school... You know magic tricks for friends... and then I did a lot of theater."

Greg Taylor possesses the sheen of aristocracy, like Augustine, with his shimmering youth and money. Why would he sell his life for tricks? I had no choice. Tricks were all I had to sell. My songs could make you cry and weep. The spells I made were of the soul, of a man's grief and longing. Tricks of the heart.

I remember dawns alone in the cafés, after men and women had gone home with bellies full of wine and bread, their heads full of music. I had my voice only, strained and tired as the sun rose. Angelica brought beauty to my sad songs as she danced to them—danced without exhaustion—her hands widening to the rays of early morning. Ah, that was magic.

"Ever disappear before?"

"Disappear? No," he stands close to her, his hands on his hips.

"Good...let me teach you."

"Psst." I hear from a corner behind the stage. "Carlos." It is Saint Michael dressed in black pants, topless, like the young Greg Taylor. His skin is rich and brown, like mine, blending almost into the dark of the dim world behind the stage.

"Come here," he motions at me with his finger. His generous wings reach into the mysterious heights above the stage with its pulleys and ropes. He whispers, "What a coincidence!" and then smiles ironically. "The man who came to help her when you could not kill her. Isn't this exciting, Carlos! It's been ages since I've seen a good magic show." Saint Michael picks up a saw resting against a wooden box. "Magicians cut people in half." He winks his eye. "You know that, Carlos?"

"Yeah... yeah... I know. I know," I say turning away from him looking out into the theatre, catching sight again of the girl.

"Who is she?" I whisper.

"No need to whisper. They can't hear a word... the girl?"

"She's the one I couldn't kill... it's her. Did I know her in my former life? Was she Angelica? Patia?"

Saint Michael walks to a table with two chairs on either side, squeezed into a corner surrounded by planks of wood and rolls of fabric.

"Here, sit. You met her without knowing it, but you changed her life forever."

"For good?" I ask, but I know the answer. I must have brought evil to her. I did very little good in those days.

Saint Michael points his palm upward. "Look."

He sends the light of the lunar table onto the wall behind us. Flavia my sister appears. She has uneven teeth and a long face. Her eyes seem to hang.

"She had a hard heart," he says shaking his head.

I nod and then hear the words.

"Grandma put poison in your dinner. She wants to get rid of you. You'll be dead soon." She grabs my shoulder and throws me out the door. She points to the hole outside the door where I sleep when I am naughty. "Now, lie down. This is where you will die." I crouch into the ground, but when she leaves, I run into the vineyards, and then hide from all of them, beneath the curling vines as the summer sky darkens. I am four years old. A life already of lies and betrayals.

I know what death is. I have seen animal carcasses in the open graves near the meadow. The eyes of dead goats are eaten by little bugs. Death is what took my mother and my uncle Juan. I stare into the sky.

Death is coming, Carlos. Watch out, death is walking

from the fields to get you. The air is warm and smells of manure and straw roasted by the sun, hot and decaying. I want to crawl to Patia inside the house, ask her to carry me, keep me from slipping into my grave. But I am forbidden from entering the house. So all night, I listen for the steps of death while the snoring dogs wheeze and the crickets chant. What does death sound like? I fall asleep before the cock crows. My mouth opens to a rock near my teeth sucking at it like a breast. When I hear the rooster sing, I open my eyes. Am I in heaven? I look around and see the familiar land. I am relieved, but not too much, for life is miserable here. I look out at the horizon to the rays of a new morning.

I am a sad-eyed boy, from the gypsy people, humming to grapes as the sun rises. How can anyone believe that I am anything else? My father is wrong, my grandmother. I have no payo blood in me. I am dark-skinned and missing two teeth. I wear the hat of my grandfather, the brim sinks below my eyebrows. A melody rises from the hollow of my scarred lips as flies buzz near the vines.

"All your misery was built on what people believed about you . . . although none of it was true," Saint Michael says. "So you found your own private truth in music."

"That's right," I sigh, "in my own private world."

When I am little, I sneak into the bodegas, and hide under the arching roofs. I look up at the brown beams, feel the cool floor beneath me and listen to the world outside. I hear dogs fighting, their feet scratching at the rocky soil. I hear growls of old men barking back. Doves coo on our roofs with free throats, the hands of those who are not gypsies, payos, lift them into the wind in celebration of the harvest.

But it is not just noise that draws me, but the forbidden hum of a world inside where I am king, and the others around me die. For it is in that private space between my ears where I hear the doves sing, or the presses outside squeeze the grape, in that world of sounds and melodies that others do not know where I reign and my tear-filled songs become shouts against injustice.

While the payos celebrate the mesto, the pressed juice of the grape, gypsies sing songs in honor of fingers so numb they no longer begin or end, knuckles that bend without thinking and cannot straighten for hours. I find comfort in my own voice as it fills with tears. I sing to myself about the heat and hunger after beatings.

I sing of revenge for the suffering I know, as a gypsy and an outcast from my own family.

One day, I am drawn to a brimming basket of grapes because I am so hungry and thirsty. I steal a bunch, and that is a small crime for every grape is money to a gypsy, and every coin needed. But I sink my teeth into the sweet fruit with the tension of a starving man, and I am caught by my grandmother. She ties me to a tree and hits me while the others watch, shaking their heads, knowing that I am no good. I sour with every strike against me, sour like a rotting fruit. The boy who grabs grapes is like a thief who steals money from his family. I find music in the pain and sing as I sleep alone in the dark. I am your bad fruit.

I am your bad fruit.

"Magic is a wonderful thing," Saint Michael chuckles. "Isn't it great to be fooled by a trick. It's all so innocent, really!"

3.

THE FLOWERING VEIL

Virgen de la Macarena
Reflejo de luna dara
Da en tu crita morena
No hay cara como tu cara
Ni peña come tu peña.

Virgin of Macarena
The bright moon's reflection
Shines in your dark little face
There is no face like yours
And no pain like your pain.

Saint Michael sleeps in a corner backstage. He is spread out on the floor, his wings forming a soft bed beneath him. The hum of an angel's snores softens his mouth. I once imagined he was like the other angels with their rigid backs and conforming, judging eyes. But he is not. There is mischief in his sleeping face. He has slept on the floors of many houses, it seems; his back holds the memory of calluses, having shaped itself to stone, mud, the cold cracked tile of a stranger's room.

He is at home like this, close to the Earth with his dreaming. I imagine him as a bandit, like me, roaming the hills near Cádiz for treasures, clutching at the rocky slopes with hoofed feet. Saint Michael was once like me—in one lifetime, at some point in history. I am sure of it.

I walk away from him into the darkened theatre. The others are all gone, but the two of them. Greg Taylor pulls his shirt back on over his head. Jeannie, the magician, stands close to him. It must be good to face a woman like that with her body close.

Isn't it clear? Fate has brought these two together, and this old Death Angel is a pawn in some game of love. I don't understand what God wants of me here, so I listen, following their voices as they travel down the empty aisles. I am an Angel of Death. All I know of love I learned from Angelica. The angels have taught me little. But I remember those days in Spain when Angelica widened my lips and left me like a fool with a mouth open for her. Hah!

"How did you get into this?" Greg asks the girl.

"What?"

"Magic . . . escaping from bottles..."

"I fell in love with magic when I was a kid. I loved making people go, 'Wow!'... The power of illusion..."

"I'm curious about something. When I found you... you were babbling away at something, someone."

That was me, I whisper, *Carlos Peña.*

"Really? I don't remember that. But the mind does things under stress. I rely on it—rely on the mind's ability to..."

"You were staring up and looking like you were talking to someone..."

She walks towards the door, "Yeah? I don't remember..."

"You don't?" He reminds me of the Spanish choir boys so clean they scrubbed their gums.

"The mind's power to create illusions. Understand? We like illusions. We find them entertaining, and when we're under stress, they help us."

Greg steps away from her and looks out around the theatre at the empty seats, "How do you know that everything people see is an illusion?"

"Well, there are a lot of people like you who think there is something going on... I mean like supernatural, but I think hallucinating is the most natural thing for the mind to do and explains just about everything I have ever heard about. About two years ago — maybe you heard — I did the Jeannie in the Bottle trick in the plaza downtown, trying to break Rick Foster's record for staying underwater."

"Yeah, yeah, I remember that. It got a lot of press."

"Anyway, so I was just getting past six minutes and I was aiming for seven, and I am thinking, 'Shit. This is getting hard...' and then something happened, it was as if all thought just disappeared and I began becoming part of the water. Like not working against the water but blending with it. My breath and the water became one entity— and suddenly, I felt the presence of two sea animals next to me. And I know this sounds crazy, but one was this sea anemone who was breathing for me, and then on the other side, was this beautiful angel fish, full of electric colors, and I relaxed into them, and went on a kind of trip with them. That occupied my mind from my fear and gave me this deep relaxation... I just went with..." She rolls her eyes, "the flow..."

"That's amazing."

"But what was that? It was my mind—nothing supernatural about it... just totally natural but amazing, right? It is how the mind is. Our minds imagine all kinds of things to help us get through stuff or to entertain us. I rely on the human mind's love for illusion. That is the key to a good trick. We all want to believe in magic... Don't you?"

"Not everything is a trick...or even a hallucination."

"Really? Why do you want it to be anything else than it is? Why does it have be more than the imagination? The imagination is great, a power beyond anything—that is what magic is about—the great power of our minds to live in illusion and imagination. I don't really understand why we have to make something more of it."

"You don't believe in anything like ghosts?"

"I've spent my life proving they don't exist," she walks towards the exit.

"Maybe you were visited by a ghost. Maybe somehow that spirit kept you and your car from going across the railing and falling into the sea."

"Are you on some kind of mission?"

He shrugs his shoulders, "What do you mean?"

"What's the big deal with you and ghosts?"

"I've always believed in them, can even sense them, the dead. Like now. I feel a presence in the room. I'm wondering if someone has a message for you."

"Message?" She looks at him. "I don't know what you mean."

But Greg is unmoved. "Are you really so skeptical?"

"I am an illusionist. I know better. And besides, I do bring back the dead..."

"You do?"

"Séances at the Crimson Lady—For $35 a person, I can make the dead come back."

"But that's not real," Greg pouts. "You're taking advantage of people."

"I don't see it that way. I put on a good show—and every penny I earn from my séances goes to poor kids for college..."

"You're still taking advantage.."

"For a good cause. Come on, Greg. Everyone wants to believe. What kid refuses the idea of Santa Claus? A magician lives off of other people believing. You'll understand if you land up working for me. The world is a mechanical place."

"You don't believe in anything?"

"It's not a matter of believing... it's a matter of accepting life's terms. I believe in the five senses, you know... and I know about the power of imagination... That's a wonderful thing... really... now that's the magic I believe in."

Maybe she was once my Angelica with her chin pointed forward, never looking back. Oh that woman's will! But Angelica did believe in something more, something that was gypsy, as dark as the red wine at the bottom of the barrel with its swollen bouquet. The soul, the heat of duende. It was not illusion. Grown men would weep at the sight of a woman possessed by duende. Duende made people cry, collapse, tear at their shirts.

Duende is the magic of death; it changes a room in a matter of minutes with the ever-presence of the portal as it opens to a world beyond. Hija dance, dance for me with those spinning shoulders! Turn your body into a snake! La Culebra, she was mine once! That is the magic of a gypsy!

Real magic.

Jeannie locks the doors as they exit into the cold and windy streets. I look up at the theatre's small marquee, the lights darkened. Jeannie puts her hand on Greg Taylor's shoulder, "You'll be great on stage. See you tomorrow."

He nods, wordless, as he braces against the angry winds. I watch the two as they walk in separate directions into the almost stormy night. I slip back into the theatre where Saint Michael stands on stage, his arms stretched in front of him. He is acting to an empty audience, reciting words into the echoing theatre.

"Shakespeare—you know him, don't you?"

I do not say anything. I am a gypsy, and I am not stupid, but names like these are only words to me.

"We were friends in the 16th century, a hell of a writer. I acted for him. Now that was one of my better lives."

"I bet it was," I say, looking around, wondering why I cannot remember all my lives. It as if I am chained still to that one time, those hot summers in Spain, the cooling Nevada winters, that life of suffering and music of a gypsy.

"We can remember it all," he says, as if knowing my thoughts, "when we're done. All those lifetimes line up one after another like chapters in a great book, like Shakespeare. Take a look, okay, Carlos? Now, come, gypsy boy, let's go see Flora."

He leads me again to the corner backstage and guides me to the chair. "Sit here."

"Shouldn't we go back to heaven?" I feel uncomfortable here in this dark and crowded space, the cables and pulleys above my head seem to move in the dark.

"Who needs heaven? We're angels. Any place is heaven to us, right, Carlos?" I look around in the dark, and then there is an explosion of light against the wall. A face of a beautiful woman stares out at me from the lunar table.

"Flora?" She looks almost nothing like the grandmother I hated.

"Yes, Carlos, when she was young. Still beautiful, but you look closely. You can see the face of a woman whose heart is closing."

I never knew there was beauty in her. Her eyes are brown and black like those of a calf with long sleepy lids. She stands sadly facing a wall, with an open mouth, her hands clasped stiffly in front of her.

"She's so young here," I say. Her chin is straight, her jaws meet without twisting. There is no scar, just a plane of smooth skin. She is not the Flora I know, but a woman with plump lips, lips that I could imagine kissing. She wears a white cotton dress that sticks to her; it must be summer, for she is hot, and fear forms pools of sweat on her back and beneath her breasts. Six gypsy men sit at the table. It is a *kris*, a gypsy tribunal.

"The first law," says one of the council, a balding senior, "a wife must be faithful to her man. Betray a man, you betray your people—understand?"

She must not turn around; her gaze is filthy. She has sinned against God and the gypsies.

"You misuse beauty, you lose beauty," says another man. "That is our ruling." He stands with a whip in his hand. He is the tallest of them with long arms and a full head of hair.

Suddenly, the whip strikes, ripping her skin, leaving a gash from ear to chin. Flora's palms rush to her jaw as if to catch it, as if it is falling to pieces. The whip cracks one more time on her hands and cheek, letting loose a gush of blood that empties onto her throat. She falls to her knees, curled in pain.

"Yes," she says, her hands curled into fists.

"We cannot allow this," the balding man says without squeamishness.

"Yes," Flora replies, her words muffled by her swollen mouth, the jaw now hanging unevenly. "Yes." She cries but only softly, swallowing down the salt of blood and sorrow.

"Will you be faithful now—if he takes you back?" asks the older man.

"Yes," she lifts her bloodied face.

"Now you've met with justice—bring in Rodolfo."

Grandfather walks in. His hair is still black, not one thread of gray, and only a few lines are scorched into his face by the sun. The shoes click onto the floor echoing as he looks down at his bleeding wife. Her eyes plead with him as her fingers rest on the open wound.

"Rodolfo, will you take her back?" asks the man with the whip.

Rodolfo walks to the open window and searches the sky for the answer. Click. Click. He comes towards her again. She looks, her neck stretches, eyes full of sorrow, for she loves him.

"I will never betray you again, Rodolfo, I promise."

He circles her, each time coming closer, like a great eagle who watches the snake. Her lips swell. The cheeks slowly bruise.

"You may come home," he says clicking his tongue. He is full of disgust, his bottom lip curls in hatred.

"I will do all you say," she vows.

My grandmother's jaw will hang in its shame forever and her twisted mouth will never forget. No other man will want her again. She will now be La Cicatriz, The Scar. When she dances for strangers, she will try to turn her face, so that all who see her can only see the cheek that has not been scarred, that is still innocent. Walking home, my grandfather leads his wife by the hand. She follows slowly behind him, head down, like a mule. He whistles and then sings, "Each time I think of you, I wish I were never born, or that you were never born."

I press my hand to my chest and sigh deeply. It is the first time I have known Flora's pain.

"So," says Saint Michael, "Flora could not escape her own conscience, her shame. She saw her sin in her daughter."

"Yes, I see that, but still I . . ."

"Wait, there's more. One year before you were born." I glance up at the lunar table again. Gray clouds carry the smell of rain. Every year it is the same, in February, the house floods with water. The wind rattles the empty vines. Across the cultivated fields near the river is a woman. It is my mother. Her black hair has been let loose by the wind and it flies in its gusts.

Patia, Sara and Flavia are at her feet. She stands close to a Spaniard, Paulo. He owns the vineyards where my family works. He has light skin, as light as straw, and he is short and lean, dressed in tight black pants and a new cotton shirt. When Rosa's hair rides the breeze, he gently pulls it from her face, so he can see her more clearly, see her dark skin, the crack of her mouth when she speaks.

Flora watches all from her open door on the other side of the vineyards. She cannot see everything, but enough. Love's magnet pulls. So it seems. And then the storm comes. Rain dashes itself on the dry earth with the fury of a broken heart. Rosa opens her palms to gather the children. The Spaniard puts his hand on her shoulder and leads them into one of the buildings. They run hip to hip, escaping into the dry walls where most gypsies are forbidden, into Paulo's elegant rooms where the bosses sip sherry and balance ledgers.

Flora, La Cicatriz, stands in front of her house in the pouring rain. She does not move at all except to keep her eye on Rosa as she disappears into Paulo's small palace. The rain soaks Flora's clothes and the cold air pulls her hair from its bun. But she stands there, waiting. The pellets of rain do not move her. Her eyes are tied to Paulo's closed door, to the windows and walls that keep out the cold. There is only one fate for an adulteress. Flora waits anxiously for Rosa and the children to leave Paulo's house. There are no signs. Flora stands until every strand of hair is drenched in the cold juice of winter, until she has no strength left.

The men come home with scraps of wood to cover the windows, but it will not be enough. It never is. Rain will come in through the cracks of the floor and dampen everything.

"Where's Rosa... the girls?" Eduardo asks.

"She's run an errand for Paulo," Flora says.

"You're a mess," grandfather pulls at her hair. "What are you doing in the rain? Get inside. We need dinner."

She dries herself with her one sweater and then makes bread. Her hands sink into the cold dough while the men hang the wood into the open windows to keep out the cool drops. Rosa trots in almost an hour later through the door, shaking off the rain. Her hair is braided with new ribbon. The girls dance, twirling their skirts as if they are also new. Eduardo eyes them coolly.

"Where have you been?" he asks.

"Paulo gave us soup," Flavia says.

"Paulo?" Eduardo walks over to Rosa with threats in his steps. "What were you doing there?"

"He's kind to us," Rosa says.

"He let us sit near his fire," Sara nods.

"If he's so good, why does he let our houses fill with water?" Eduardo tightens the wood onto an old hook with twine. "If he's so good, where's my damned soup?" Eduardo slaps Rosa's face and warns her. "He's no friend. He gives us nothing for our work so that he can live like a king."

This is how it is in the land where we live, in those times, those days. A man is always right and has his suspicions. The children run to the corner and sit, for they have learned that they must be silent when their father is angry. Flora pulls at the dough with her cracked skin.

Even for a woman, tears are a sign of weakness. Rosa sheds none, but glares at her husband. "I am sorry," she says without meaning it, her hand curled to her stinging cheek. "I am sorry, Eduardo."

The image fades as another appears on the lunar table. It must be early spring, for the sun is full, but the wind is still strong.

"Months before your birth," Saint Michael whispers.

Rosa does not yet show the full moon of her pregnant belly. She washes clothes in the river near the small patch of meadow where the children play. Paulo appears. This time he stands with his hat in his hands, and Rosa speaks to him with lively arms as she would with her own family. Flora looks up from the cooking pit outside past the cultivated fields where the two are speaking. Flora sits first with the stillness of a cat watching its prey, then slinks down into the flowering vineyards as Paulo walks away.

"Don't think it," Flora says sharply, her feet approaching her unsuspecting daughter.

"What?" Rosa startles as she turns.

"I know. Do you think I am stupid? I can see what is

between you and Paulo."

"What?"

"I have the gift of seeing. I know what you are doing."

Rosa stands with her palms on her hips and shakes her head, "What are you talking about?"

"I have paid," says Flora, "and so will you."

"What are you talking about, mother?"

"This scar."

"The scar?" Rosa asks. Her mother has never spoken of it before.

"You have been warned," Flora walks away, leaving dust behind her.

"But your mother never sinned," Saint Michael rises to his feet. "Oh, she teased and toyed with Paulo, but she never acted on her desire."

"Are you sure?" I ask.

"Yes, Carlos. I am sure."

"So my grandmother was wrong. It was all wrong . . . all of it?"

I laugh at the sad truth. I laugh but I am almost crying because it is funny and cruel at the same time. I was believed to be the Spaniard's son. A gypsy child with the blood of a Spaniard is cursed, condemned to face the world alone. I was double-cursed because my mother was suspected of being unfaithful. For a gypsy baby, there is no curse worse than a mother who has loved a payo and loved him outside of gypsy marriage. So on the eve of my birth, Flora and Eduardo awaited me, suspecting I was tainted, the plump white fish, made of an outsider's blood. Eduardo left because he believed Flora. My mother's memory was soiled. I was treated like a demon conceived in sin, a little devil pushed out between Rosa's thighs.

"When Rosa died, it was taken as a sign from God that your mother was unfaithful," Saint Michael says. "But you know how death really is Carlos. Rosa died, she just died. God brought her home. It was no punishment. In truth, she was faithful to your father."

"And all those years of hate," I say, "for no reason . . ."

"No reason at all," Saint Michael says. "Except for the veil." He walks towards away from me towards the magician's theatre.

"The veil?" I ask, standing up, following him.

"Of perception—we see the world through the veil of our own experience. Many of us do not see what the world really is. Just how we really are." He stands on the stage and looks out.

"But that's no excuse," I say.

"Of course not. What Flora did was wrong. Her suffering colored everything."

My thoughts then turn to my life in the cramped rooms of Cádiz where children and their parents had so little to eat and died of diseases that turned their skin yellow and knotted their fingers in pain and fever.

"But the world is so terrible sometimes," I say.

"Of course it is, but we make choices. We can let suffering turns us toward evil or..."

"Toward love." I finish his sentence but do not quite believe this. I know it is the right thing to say, but I cannot imagine with all the suffering of my life that I could have chosen love. I lived through the veil of hatred, I know that, but when you are young or the pain is too much, it seems there is no choice.

"But when you are suffering," I say, "it's hard to choose love." I am thinking now of myself, not Flora.

He says, "Exactly. Flora was asleep, she just acted. And so were you. You two were not that different."

My chest hardens with these words. Not that different? Flora ruined me. But then I think of the Home for the Poor and the ashes I left behind, Piedro and his bloodied throat, Angelica weeping in a room as I stood there just watching. I ruined lives with my evil, I know this. Saint Michael walks down the stairs to the left of the stage and motions for me to follow him.

"You were young, Carlos," he stands waiting.

"Yes, I was."

"And you deserved none of it. But she was like the adult you became. It all came from pain."

"I see that now," I say. "It's like the flowering veil." I am thinking aloud, seeing the images of the large barrels, and imagining the thin sheath of yeast. "The veils that protect the sherry from the air outside . . ."

"That's right. Our veils protect us, but also do us harm. Your grandmother never knew you or even her own daughter. She only knew herself, her own pain, for everything she saw was through that veil."

"You understand though," I say, "why I hated her . . . why I had all these terrible thoughts in my head, and why the day Flora died, I felt free."

"Of course I understand," says Saint Michael, leading me out. He wraps his arm around my shoulder and points to the doors as they close. "Who knows more about the veils of illusion than a magician? But who knows less about truth?" He starts to laugh, his throat widening, his head falling back. He laughs and laughs.

I hear his laughter still even as I settle back into heaven, into the executioner's quarters with the howling grief of the jackals outside my window, with the rising of that lonely moon, the eye of God watching me, watching as I sleep.

4.
THE SEANCE

Desgracio de aquel que vive y
Come pan de mano ajena
Siempre mirando a la cara
Si la pone mala o buena.

Unfortunate, he who has to live
By taking bread from another's hand
Who always has to check the face
To see if it approves or disapproves.

Angelica's grandmother is Juana. She sees fortunes in stone. People come from miles to ask her what she sees in the cradle of the rocks. "The Earth is wise. In all its pebbles are the answers to every question. You just need to look. Look, Carlos."

I see nothing but ridges and dust, but Juana sees it all. I am just a boy, but I always listen closely when Juana tells my future.

"Beware of strangers and find love away from home. You have a sad destiny, Carlitos, but you can sing, so you do not need good luck."

It was true, I could sing, and more true that I had a bad fate.

Juana knows the truth about Carlos, about my past in the Home for the Poor in the days before I come to live with her and Angelica. But Juana never says anything. The knowledge is in her eyes, not in her tongue.

Juana brings back the dead. On Sunday nights the payos come and leave a few pesetas in the bowl for the gifted gypsy. She calls out to the spirits, and the windows shake with their arrival. Their ghostly breath rises from her mouth while her fat body is a solid mountain grounded by the roots of her feet.

Juana leads real séances so the dead can speak. This girl, Jeannie, just plays tricks.

She is seated at the head of a table, in a back room of a seaside restaurant. She is wearing a copper wig and her face is thickly painted.

"Our girl is playing gypsy," Saint Michael whispers to me as we rest in the rafters, pretending to hear the dead ..."

"Why does she look that way?" I ask, half repulsed.

"It's a kind of disguise." Saint Michael leans into my ear to whisper. "She must hide her true identity. No one can know she is a magician by trade. Tricks only work when we are deceived."

"Ladies and gentleman. Thank you so much for joining me in tonight's séance at the Crimson Lady," the magician says.

Saint Michael listens, his chin on his palm. A woman in her forties sits to the left of the girl, wearing a gray felt hat that droops like her sad face; two men, they seem to be brothers, sit leanly beside her. "We are an intimate group tonight. Spirits are more comfortable in these smaller séances."

I roll my eyes. Saint Michael nudges me, eyes twinkling with delight, "Theatre, Carlos, theatre!"

The room darkens.

Jeannie takes a deep breath and asks that everyone join hands. "Bless this room, surround us in heavenly light." I see no dead anywhere around us. But then even I am fooled for a moment. A ray of light glides across the table. The woman with the hat lets out a small gasp.

"What's that?" I ask Saint Michael. "How does she do it."

"Simple earth mechanics, Carlos. A projector hidden over there."

"Projector?"

The magician says, "I am hearing something now. There is someone with us." She closes her eyes. "Please identify yourself."

The room is quiet, thick with concentration.

"There is a presence with us now... first name begins with an E...Is it Ev—Ev-..."

The woman raises her hand shyly. "I think he's for me...

my brother... my brother Everet."

"He tells me. Wait. He tells me to tell you that he is okay—not to worry anymore."

"Oh, thank God."

"He says to tell Mar—Mar—"

"Martha?" the woman asks.

"Yes, Martha, that he will always be beside her and not to worry."

"How does she know?" I ask Saint Michael. I think of Juana and the rattling windows. Was that all show too?

"Simple, research, Carlos. Anyone can do it nowadays."

"Research? What do you mean?"

"Isn't it something?" Saint Michael laughs. "But illusion's not enough for the magic of life, is it Carlos?"

"Is she lying to them?" I ask.

"She creates a life of building illusions--"

Greg Taylor walks into the Crimson Lady. There is that polished face of the boy who thinks he saved Jeannie Price on the day I failed my duties as a Death Angel.

Ah, he must have been Augustine with the smell of privilege. I am certain of it.

"I am here for the séance," Greg Taylor tells the waiter.

"The séance began 10 minutes ago."

"She is expecting me. I need to go in."

"He was Augustine?" I whisper. "Wasn't he?"

"No," Saint Michael pulls me close to him, his hand on

my shoulder. "Patience."

"Sorry I am late." Greg draws the chair close to our girl, the illusionist.

"Very distracting," her eyes pop open.

"And who was she?" I ask Saint Michael.

"You'll find out soon enough, Carlos." Saint Michael squeezes my shoulder, "Enough of these theatrics, let's go."

I follow him outside to a sand dune near the shelter of a cypress tree. He pats the ground , inviting me to sit. "It's time for a little chat about your magician."

"Jeannie?"

"Yes—Your job is to help him."

"Who? Greg?" I ask.

"Yes...You will help him love her."

It seems such a fragile thing. How can Carlos Peña, an Angel of Death be a muse for love—so many years condemned as an executioner?

"Can she even love?" I ask.

"We all can love," Saint Michael says. "Even you, Carlos Peña. But it begins first with you, peeling away the veils... so you can live through your innocent heart again. Do you remember when you first gave it up, gave up your innocence."

My chest sinks. "Home for the Poor—no?"

"Yes. You lost faith in God in the Home of the Poor... lost faith in love," Saint Michael moves close to me.

"Faith in their god," I say, putting aside the memory of Greg's golden face for an older memory of the dark building in Cádiz. As a little boy, I trusted thieves more than the priests who took care of me. A thief only wants bread. Clergy are in search of souls.

"But I was six, seven, eight years old. I was a boy, not a saint. I wanted love, but so many things happened against me. Who prayed for Carlos Peña and his pain?"

Saint Michael presses his palm into mine. The white sphere fills the tree trunk in front of us as a wind rattles the twigs that grow from it.

"Let's go back there, Carlos."

Jérez, 1890.

My grandmother Flora is dead.

Father Ference has come all the way from Cádiz to send her away. He stands there, larger than any of us, with arms that are thick with black hair that grows like spiders. He has a round face with a covering of beard and his belly is plump. His wide lips make him look like a monkey. He leads us in prayer with the words: "Flora was a holy woman." He is a good priest, grandmother told us many times, he takes care of all people, including gypsies.

But he is so big, I do not trust him. And I do not trust any man who holds a Bible in his hand. I suspect the words of a God who created my grandmother. She prays every day, and I wonder what kind of God would grant her cruel wishes? As she is lowered into the earth, I watch the tears of my sisters and my grandfather. I try to cry, try to find sadness in my heart for her death, but instead I see justice in her passing: My God has answered me. The Earth is a gigantic mouth and my grandmother goes into it.

In my dreams that night, her fingers rise out of the grave. I scream. Her hand tugs at my ankle, pulls at me, holds me, so I cannot run. It is a hand seeking revenge. The wrist bends, pulling me into the deep hole where she lies.

"Let me go! Let me go!" My screaming wakes everyone, but only Patia comes to comfort me.

"What's wrong?" She says under the light of stars. "What are you dreaming, Carlos?"

"She is coming back to get me!" I say.

"Who?"

"Abuela's not dead. We made a mistake. Pull her out. She is not dead!"

"Shhh," says Patia. "She is dead, Carlos."

"Forever?" I ask.

"Yes."

"She's mad at me."

"They're just dreams."

Grandfather sits outside beneath a tree. He has been up all night. He rocks with the lonely beat of his laments. He sings songs full of endless sorrow.

The earth has swallowed
the one woman I loved
now she is gone.

He sings with a voice that is tired and rough but cannot stop, for singing is like praying to a cantaor and the throat opens to divine sorrow.

"She won't come back?" I ask Patia.

"Only for forgiveness."

"Are you sure?"

"I am sure," Patia says.

Patia puts my sleepy body down. "Get some rest." She presses a kiss into my throat and walks away. The sky shifts to the right, and then the left, and all the stars shake out like salt around me. I am afraid. Grandfather has told me that they will be leaving in the morning for Granada to find my real father, Eduardo. But I will be left behind. I cannot go with them because my father does not want me. I am everything in life that is betrayal, born of his wife's imagined infidelity. Besides, I am one more hungry mouth to feed, the youngest, the weakest. The runt. Sometimes I fear I have no skin, just bones. In the morning, we begin our sojourn to Cádiz by rented horses, by diligencia, gathering other riders and their things, traveling across the rocky hillsides to the port of Cádiz.

"He is my brother, you cannot take him away," Patia says to grandfather, seated on horseback as I curl around her.

The winds of spring come from the sea.

"Grandmother is dead and I am old, Patia. We must find your father, but Carlos cannot come with us."

"Carlos is my brother. I will go where he goes." The sunlight gathers in her dark hair.

"It will be better there, Patia." the old man says. "He will be with other orphans."

"He's my brother," she says, looking back at me, the rhythm of horse hooves gives her words power. "He belongs with us."

We arrive in the city that will be my new home: Cádiz. I've never seen such a place with its crowded streets near the ocean. There is a seaside promenade where merchants lay out large burlap bags with amber and topaz rings, freshly dried herbs and glittering pots and incense burners. Perfumed smoke wanders the air. Cut gardenias float in glass bowls as girls bend down to smell them. The large ships with their tall masts rock with the waves. Monkeys from far lands jump in the branches of trees while lovers of all ages walk beneath trellises overflowing in jasmine and honeysuckle. I want to be running free here on these streets of Cádiz where the sea is. Instead, we head down a narrow road past the dome of a white church to a darkening alley.

"It's down here," our guide points. I look up at the large stone building, crowded into the cobble-stoned street. The horses stop. Grandfather pulls me from the horse, and gestures that I should walk the steps to the door of the large black stone building and knock.

My hand pounds the thick door. "Why do I have to go?" I ask again, looking back.

"It's how it is," Grandfather says. "We can do no better for you, son. I am sorry. We have so little. You will have more here in the Home for the Poor."

The large doors open. Father Ference walks out, looks down at me with a smile and then whispers into my grandfather's ear. Patia pulls again at my hand, "We'll see each other again," she says. "I know we will."

Grandfather hugs me, "Now do what is right, Carlos."

Patia tightens her body around me. "See you later," she says. She is fourteen now and already sees the future.

Grandfather presses me into his rough cheeks. They stiffen as they keep tears away. "We are sorry, boy, but this is best for all. May God be with you."

I look back at the small caravan: several rented horses, my grandfather's burro, my three sisters, large canvas, leather sacks and my grandfather crumpled up, waving good-bye. Three strangers have traveled with us since Jérez, and they watch with pity. But Flavia and Sara have no sadness in their hearts. They stand like barren trees, hands like dead branches fluttering in the wind as they wave to me. I imagine all the heartless things they say. Even as I walk into the dark building, I know they fill each other's ears with tales about Carlos Peña. I am only six, but this is how it is: My life is built on the lies others tell about me. The door closes on their faces, and I am there, in the cool dark halls of the Home for the Poor.

I turn, thinking of Patia, ready to break out to her, like a horse in the wide open fields of the countryside. Instead, I see the large wooden door, unlabeled, no sign or even a cross as it slams shut. I look down at the stone floor, cobbled and brown beneath me.

"Sit down, Carlos. Sit down, please," Father Ference smiles. His lips stretch to show the pink of his gums. But I do not smile back. Men drift by in long brown gowns with twined rope knotted around their hips, carrying the weight of small brown crosses, like penises of horses hanging down. They all pass by quietly, heads nodding. These are not the priests I have seen in the plazas wearing black, their large-brimmed hats tilting as they look down at the children gathered at their mothers' feet.

These men wear brown robes and some even speak in accents. They have a secret, and it is in the air, in the quiet. Monks, all boys and men, pass by and look at me: one more orphan.

5.
HOME FOR THE POOR

Cuatro casas tiene puertas abiertas
Para El que no tiene dinero:
El hospital y la carcel,
La iglesia y el cementerio.

There are four homes with open doors
For the man who has no money:
The hospital, the jail
The church, and the cemetery.

Father Ference's belly is fat and his feet shuffle with the extra weight. I imagine his legs are pale and thick, and I wonder what he eats to make him that way. I have never seen a man of such mass. In Jérez, the old women sometimes got fat from too many children or their breasts plumped with milk. But there was not a man like this, so full of weight.

"Carlos, Carlos. You're our twentieth."

"Oh," I say. I do not understand what twentieth means.

"We have nineteen boys here now," he clarifies for me, but it still makes no sense. I do not know numbers. Father

Ference is trying to be kind. My skin feels tight and too brown, and I am very hungry. Flora is dead, and I could be home now, dancing in vineyards with Patia or sleeping beneath the stars without Flora's angry words. Instead I am standing at the belly of a man whose hands are curved from years of clutching Bibles.

"Brother Lorenzo will get everything arranged for you." His words slow with the slur of a tongue so wide it cannot escape its own teeth. "I see Flora in your face." He puts his finger beneath my chin and smiles again. I cannot get the muscles of my face to join his. He is Flora's priest. His God is her God, not mine.

"It will be different here," Father Ference explains. He says that they will teach me to live like a payo. I will have to give up my gypsy ways. "You will read, Carlos. You will write. You will know that there is more to life than free wandering." He sputters as he loses breath.

A young friar comes into the lobby where I sit. He has a baby's face and fumbling hands that hold a piece of paper.

"Lorenzo will take care of you," Father Ference nods his head.

"Do everything he says."

"Yes, sir." My words are whispered. Wet with hunger, they are obedient for the sake of a starving gut.

Father Ference walks down the hall. I watch the drift of his ass under his robe. Lorenzo reads from the wrinkled sheet in his hand. I see only bursts of air and a young mouth with white teeth that opens and closes. This is how it is for me as a boy. Sometimes I become deaf and only hear a song that grows power inside me. It is a strange crackling hymn, a hum, like the fire in a forest that cracks at the trees. Later I will learn the rules Lorenzo reads to me:

1. No singing before 6 a.m., during siesta or after 8 p.m.

2. Only children of 12 years or under can be punished with smacking.

3. Attend Mass with the greatest of cleanliness, composure, silence and devotion.

4. After rising each morning, give thanks to God for the good you have received.

5. Whenever you pray, do so in a loud voice, so your prayers can be heard.

6. Wake up at 5:30 a.m., be dressed, washed and hair brushed by 6 a.m.

7. Between 6 and 7 a.m. in the morning find out what your tasks are for the day, along with schedule of classes.

8. Go to morning mass.

9. At 7 a.m., have breakfast, and return to your tasks for the day until 12 noon.

10. After lunch, you will work and go to classes until 2 p.m., except for those who must do homework.

11. In the months of November, December and January, everyone must be in bed by 8:30 p.m, and at 9 p.m. the other

months.

12. The hour for Rosary will be as signaled after prayer.

"Any questions?" he asks. He must be sixteen years old, almost a man, but his skin is smooth like mine.

"No," I shake my head. I do not remember most of what he read to me. I have perfected the art of looking like I am there when I am not there at all.

The Home for the Poor has all the darkness of wine cellars. The front of the building is windowless, but the back looks out on a small orchard and courtyard where the children play.

"The building has three floors—and a wing outside," Lorenzo tells me. I can tell he has said these words many times before. There is no feeling in them. He speaks in one tone as if he has no voice of his own. "Downstairs is the kitchen and dining room. That's where some of the brothers and Father sleeps. The second floor, where we are now, has bedrooms and classrooms. Upstairs is chapel. Understand? Outside in the cottage is where I sleep with Brothers Juan, Pablo and Francisco. You sleep down the hall with the others. You are not allowed to go anywhere in the buildings without our permission. Understand?"

He motions me forward to the bedroom. Down the corridor are several classrooms. Their doors are slightly opened. As we pass, I can see small groups of boys seated at tables, eyes looking up at the hanging slates with chalk letters.

At the end of this hall is a large room with many beds. Mine is near a window that looks out at the fruit trees and the high stone walls.

Brother Lorenzo says, "Let's get you out of your old clothes, into these." He pulls my shirt over my large ears, his fingers glide against my body. I like the comfort of his hand. It pauses as he touches me, as if it has landed there. "Now wash up. It is almost time for lunch. We will be downstairs."

The voices of the boys fill the air outside. It is a sweet sound really, a sound of hope, children lost in play, children without parents under the watch of these tall priests in robes, their slow footsteps down the halls, following the shadows of boys like me, abandoned boys. I am so skinny and little. I walk the hall to the stairwell and go downstairs below. As I enter the lunchroom, there is the ring of a hand-held bell and all the orphans file slowly into the room.

An older friar leads me by the shoulder. "Peña?" he asks.

"Yes, sir," I say.

I am seated between José Pelon and Enrique Peniente.

"What's your name, runt?" José says, sticking his finger into my ribs and grinning widely.

"I am Carlos."

"Carlos?" He says, "Can you fight?"

"Yes," I say. "Yes, I can." But I am just a little boy, like a little flea on the back of a horse.

He looks at me and starts to laugh with a wild open

mouth. "You can't fight. You don't even have any meat on you. How could you fight?"

The boys joke that I am too small to fight. They say I have no muscle. Besides I am still a baby. They say that I am a gypsy, so I will never learn to read or write. The brothers do not notice that the boys tease me. There are so many hungry mouths to feed, little birds with wide beaks pushed into the air.

I look into the bowl of meat and rice, and I do what I did at home with grandmother. I no longer hear. I simply enter the secret forest. It is a place in my head where I go where all the trees are tall, and I can look up and see a roof made of leaves. Here all the world stops. I am master of this paradise. When Abuelita would throw me outside, I would imagine my secret forest, and I would go there, and set the trees on fire. One by one the flames would spread out around the branches. But the flames would never touch me. They would devour the little bunnies and the eagles, but I could just watch with the torch in hand.

At night it is worse. While we are all in bed, the boys say I am a runt and too stupid, and night after night, they talk about how I am not learning my lessons, that my eyes and hands are always wandering, that I am stupid and small. It is like the nights when my sisters gossiped about me, and I would press my palms into my ears until their chattering cruelty would stop. I tighten every muscle, and feel the sting of words but have no tongue to speak. So I go back again and again to the forest. I walk beneath the green tangle of branches. Each twig is set into a raging blaze. As the trees collapse, I jump into the flames without harm. Heat without end.

At night before dreaming, I imagine burning the clothes of the nuns who live down the road. They come sometimes to bring us food or read us stories or give us a religious lesson. I imagine nuns on fire running down the halls, breasts wobbling. I imagine nuns standing there naked, yelling, "Fire! My clothes are burning!"

I imagine the large wooden cross that Sister Lara wears being enveloped in heat.

***

The more I am teased by the boys, the more I think of the flames. Each day passes and I sit in school, Father Ference asking me to read from the book, and all I see are black ink scratches. None of it makes sense to me, and I do not care. The more I see the eyes stare down at me and hear the words, "Carlos, are you listening?" the less I listen, and the more I hear it: the slow crackling sound, the cackling yellow blaze, the heat of my hands.

They keep a lantern, candles and matches at the stairwells of each floor and also at the end of each hallway. I steal matches and hide them throughout the orphanage to use later. I hide matches beneath the rug, in the attic near the chapel, outside in the shed. The matches are like my gold, for they hold the potential heat, the yellow riches of my angry heart.

I look at Saint Michael. What does he think now? He says nothing, but feels the press of my gaze and turns to me. His face glows with the light of the lunar table. He bows his head as if to say, "I know you are there, Carlos." He brings his finger to his lips. Is he trying to keep me quiet, as they did to me there? Is this the same thing all over again? Even now am I forced to say nothing? I will not allow it.

"I had no voice," I say.

"It's true," he replies, looking for a moment like a monk with that distant face.

"It was the same thing all over again. Just like in my family. I was an outsider. No one loved me."

"I know. I understand, Carlos."

I am annoyed by his few words. "You don't understand."

"Of course I understand."

"My rage had its reasons."

"All rage has its reasons," Saint Michael says, turning to me.

One morning, when I am done sweeping and washing dishes, I do not go to mass. I tell Brother Lorenzo that I feel ill and he takes me to the bedroom. I am to stay there until mass is over. Instead I sneak outside to the pile of wood and old paper they use for the wood stove. I gather a pile of twigs and paper and hide them in the shed outside. The singing voices of the boys rise from the chapel into the treetops. I imagine the high-reaching burn as the boys sing their hymns. I imagine praises to a God of flames. The first time I do not want to do anyone harm. I just want to hear the sound of that crackling. I will wait until after dinner, when all are in bed, then sneak outside and start a fire in the steel bins outside the kitchen doors where we keep our garbage. Just a small blaze will be enough to set the fire free, it is like a melody inside that must be sung, yellow and hot, from the mouth of a boy who does not speak. It is a night like all nights. The boys gossip and as always, their words turn to Carlos Peña and his stupid ways. But this night, I do not collapse with the hurt of the words. I can even keep my palms from my ears.

When I hear the wheezing breath of sleeping boys, I get up quietly. I creep down the hall to get a lantern, and I light it. I turn down the flame, so it burns only faintly. I head down into the kitchen, then to the back door, to the shed outside. It is cold and my breath forms smoke in the air. My heart beats quickly. I open the shed quietly and pull out my kindling and search for the red canister of kerosene. I have seen Brother Juan use it to fill lanterns. I find the kerosene on the top shelf and stand on an old chair to get it. I get down and head to the garbage. With all the care and love of a mother who tends to her only child, I set the bundle into the metal bin. I pour the clear oil onto the kindling.

I strike the fire.

The small blaze begins as a crackle. Then it grows. I run up the stairs as silently as possible. My body is so light, so small that it barely leaves a trace as I walk upon the floor. I sneak back into bed. In only a matter of minutes, I hope, everything will catch fire. I wait and I wait.

Then I hear the loud cry, "¡Incendio! ¡Incendio! Fire! Fire!" I lie in bed with a smile. The boys wake up quickly and all look out the window. I stand with them innocently and watch the climbing blaze below. Father Ference, Brother Lorenzo and several of the other monks try to put out the blaze. All the boys go running down to see. Except me. I am not sure why, but I dash upwards. I grab a candle at the stairwell and run up the steps into the dim chapel. I light the candle and look at Christ, dotted in the blood and the sins of others. Outside the flames eat away at the twigs and paper. The sad eyes of Jesus stare into me.

"Fire," I hear the word one more time from outside, then there is only quiet. The same forest inside my head. The same thing: green trees, large trees growing towards the sky. And then the roar of flames within me, twig by twig, and sometimes a blue jay is caught. Its wing catches on fire. I hear the song of the jay in my head. It is like singing and crying at the same time. It is like the wailing songs of my grandfather, the horrible cry of a cantaor in grief.

"Whoever has done this will pay!" Father Ference's voice rises from the yard below. I take one last peek at the crowned Jesus, and then gallop down the stairs into bed. I lie there as if I am sleeping. But in early morning, I sneak into the kitchen, and see the charred twigs and paper. A large mound of flour is heaped on top of the burned shells of garbage in the garbage can, burned ashes mixed with the pure snow of flour. It is the first time in my life that I feel powerful.

I set a dozen more fires in the House of the Poor and for years I escape without being caught. I set fires in the kitchen, in the garbage cans, in the sinks, in the shed, in the attic, in the storage room. There are matches in every room, and I manage to find them: in the kitchen above the stove, in the study near the candleholders. For a while the matches remain at the end of each stairwell, but once the fires begin, Father Ference hides these as well. It is only a matter of stealing some and then hiding them throughout the orphanage for my use, so they are never found near me or my bed. At first I am not suspect. I am so little and young and seem so harmless. Noisy bullies at first seem the obvious arsonists. But in time, that changes.

One day, I am called into Father's office. "Brother Pablo has been complaining about you, Carlos. What is wrong with you?" he asks with that lazy tongue, like he is too tired to lift it. "We came to save you, to take care of you. You could have been abandoned to die, but is there gratitude? There is no gratitude. You are slow and do not listen. You can barely read, much less write. God blesses every child with a gift. What is yours?"

I am the one who killed his mother. I am good at destroying things.

***

"Weren't you taught to speak to those who address you?" Father Ference is used to obedience and does not understand a boy like me. He believes that the threat of hunger is enough to make a child do as he says. At one time this was true for me. Not anymore. His bloated cheeks fill with frustrated sighs. "Well, what is it that you have to offer to the world, to us here?"

"I'm good at cleaning," I say. "I can clean."

"Good," Father says. "We'll put you in the kitchen, early in the morning, to help clean up after the baker."

"Yes, sir."

"This will keep you busy and contributing to the good."

"Yes, sir."

So it is like at home. I awake early, before the singing of birds, and make my way through the dark, with the rats and the mice and the setting moon. I am at comfort in the dark before sun rises; it is the time when all is calm, when life has not yet begun, before the hurt returns, before the white faces of the boys meet me at the stairs. This is the hour when Flora would still be sleeping, when everything breathes but nothing speaks, nothing yet comes at me with words. Only the baker, Brother Juan, passes me in the morning, and he is a silent man. He seems to carry secrets of his own. We say nothing as I put away canisters of sugar and wheat, clean up his pans and wipe down kitchen counters. He just nods and sometimes puts his hand on my shoulder as if he knows something I do not know about myself. This is the time of day I like, before the sun rises and before the praises of God begin.

One morning, Brother Juan comes to wake me as he does every dawn. The room is dark and I hear the heavy breath of sleeping boys. He waits for me in the hallway as I wash up and get dressed. I walk onto the cool floor of the bathroom, but then I hear sounds outside. There's rustling, mumbling and Father Ference's booming voice, "Out of there! Get out now! Go! Go away!" I quietly run from the bathroom to look out the window.

Children's feet scramble across grass. The gypsy children have come again to steal fruit from the orchard. Father Ference's steps approach the back door. His robe rises with the breeze. A hinge creaks. Slam. Stolen oranges roll to the ground. The children have run away, but something catches my eye. Behind the short wall near the citrus trees, a figure is crouched in the dark. Once Father is inside, the shadow emerges silently, like a cat, from the dark into the moonlit grass. It is a girl, about my age, with long curling hair. I watch as she climbs the tree. She sits on the trunk, plucks fruit with her fingertips.

The baker and I walk by candlelight downstairs to the kitchen. Then I hear a noise. When Brother Juan starts working, I sneak out the door, my steps illuminated by the light inside, to see her.

The girl has large eyes that look at me, like yellow flashes, and when she sees me, ties her skirt with a knot, so the stolen oranges do not fall, and she jumps from the tree. As she lands, one bounces out.

"It's okay," I call softly. "I don't want to hurt you. I..." She races into the dark, her hair flying, with the grace and strength of an animal, of a ghost, of smoke, of something that is not human.

Angelica.

6.
HANDS

Yo me quisiera morir a ver

Si tu te ponias

Negro lutito por mi.

I would like to die just to see

If you would dress

In black for me.

    The girl I could not kill is dreaming. There is one small light on at the far corner of her room. It's a small green lamp painted in flowers. She has a large bed with generous quilts that must feel like sleeping in clouds. I look down at her—so small and bony! How did she have the power to change the course of my days?

    "Jeannie," I whisper. "Who are you?" I have spent all my hours in the afterlife only knowing the dead. I have never walked into the soul of a living human. I tremble with the thought of it.

    Saint Michael sent me to her, into the dark. "Go, go, " he said. "Get to know the girl. Teach her to love... be an inspiration."

"Inspiration?"

I put my head against her chest to listen, feel the rise and fall of her. For too long, I have stolen breath. Now I feel the pulse of lungs, and it soothes me. I have missed the hiss of life: resting within the walls of my mother, sleeping next to Patia, hearing Angelica as she dreams. We angels have no lungs, for we have no bodies, really. When you see us, what you see is only a façade, a memory, a snapshot of who we once were, but in reality, Carlos Peña is molecule without matter, a skeleton without density, muscle without the tender meat of life.

"Jeannie," I say bending down to her warm face. "Jeannie, it's me. Wake up. It's Carlos. Your Death Angel." I cradle her face and wonder where her pain lies. I no longer see beauty there, but the pointed chin of a woman who looks as if she has never been kissed. "I must bring love and song to you," I tell her, "or we will both be condemned. You to death and me to the work of bringing the dead home forever."

I get on my knees beside her and see an old pair of ballet slippers there. They are so small, looks like a child's shoes. There are no signs of children here. A gypsy dancer like Angelica could never afford shoes like these I think shaking my head. They were for French dancers only, for girls from another world. I reach out to feel Jeannie's ballerina shoes, but my hands do not move. They ache with the longing to touch again, but as a Death Angel, I can only move things that lead to the passage of the dead, such as the rosaries of the dying, the woolen blankets of the babies, the wheels of Jeannie's car. I close my hands into sad fists and stand up, turning to the sleeping girl. If I were a muse could I lift these shoes, feel their leather? Could my fingers crawl up the legs of a young dancer and feel the long line of thigh that I have forgotten, feel my drifting hands move upward into her?

Jeannie tosses again in her sleep, but as I come closer, she jumps from her dreams. "What's that?" she says aloud.

It's just me. It's all right. She stares into my eyes, but does not see me. This happens all the time with the dead and living. I take off my hat. Carlos Peña. I look at the girl I could not kill, and I am baffled. She looks so skinny and white. Not like Angelica whose resting body was a feast for my sleepless eyes. I would watch her full dark face, those lips, ebb and flow with the breath of dreams. I would imagine how many kisses I could plant on her throat and how they would bloom like midnight roses.

Jeannie stands up and walks down the hall, then pauses at hanging photos of a bearded man playing a piano. Next to him is a little girl, dressed as a ballerina, her hands arched above her head, her large teeth in a smile. "Are you here tonight?" she says. "Huh, dad? Were you with me in the car?" The next picture is of Jeannie on a swing, legs stretched out as her body tips back. The same man, only thinner, stands behind her. In another photo, he stands on a stage, his arms lifted.

"Bravo, pops," she whispers, tapping the glass. "Always the big star."

I shake my head, but Jeannie cannot see. It was me, me -- Carlos, Jeannie-- I saved you.

She walks into the empty living room. There are no plants, no fish, no cats, no babies crying. Books line up on shelves. Faces are frozen in wooden frames. Pictures. All the imprints of life, but not real life. Not like crowded gypsy rooms full of children and infants with the lingering smells of olives and garlic. There are no clapping sticks or hands outside, no tapping feet possessed by the rhythm of a dreaming heart. There are no dogs with their wet tongues licking the old men's ears or chanting crickets hidden in the stone walls.

Jeannie opens the kitchen door. She falls into a chair. She leans her elbows into the table, and presses her head into her palms. Everything sparkles with the brilliance of a snowy hill: white, white. White labels on glass bottles and metal cans. Not a crumb or a sign of a dinner made or sipped wine, no fresh herbs growing wildly against the windowsill, no mouse or cat in the corner. But the refrigerator hums. It is the only singing thing here. And when she stands to open it, there is little food. She walks to the cabinets and throws the doors open. Her hand tightens around a glass. I stand behind her, lean into her shoulder. What is the hardness of your heart? Come and we can dance near the Guadalquivir River.

She walks into the bathroom, and picks up a bottle of

pills, tossing some into her mouth. I look in the mirror at the two of us, and I do not understand at all how we were brought together. She stands with the paleness of an American girl, and I am Carlos, Angel of Death, gypsy from Jérez, tall and lean with mournful eyes, a chin of stubble, and missing teeth. My mouth opens into a grin.

Jeannie walks back to bed, and I slide in next to her. She stays awake at first, her back and neck stiff, her breath shallow. Then, little by little the neck softens and she slips into my arms. I imagine my arms are wrapped around her and my palms cup her small breasts. I crave skin again. Can Saint Michael hear these thoughts? Breathe into me, Jeannie. I pull her closer, begging her neck to give its scent to me. And then, as if she knows me, Jeannie turns and looks at me with hateful eyes. What makes her so tight like this, so fragile and rigid? She is stiff as the dead. How could anyone breathe life into this?

She turns around again so that the full spine of her back is revealed. I will possess this woman, I swear. I will possess her with the wildness of a man from another world. She rolls to the other side of the bed as if she wants to escape, and I try to roll next to her. We play a game together: the escape artist and Carlos, the Angel of Death.

My hand moves toward her one more time. "Come here, come let me feel you, girl. I will not bring you death, I promise." I look up toward the sky. What does Saint Michael see in me? I am not sure, but I have always been a man of passion, so I press a kiss into her throat, but of course, she feels nothing but the breeze of my mouth. I feel only the numbness of a Death Angel—no sweet, hot breath, no nerves in my lips, my tongue, in this ethereal body. Relax, and let me teach you how to love, I whisper, surprised by my own words. Her body softens into me, into the Angel of Death.

I think of Angelica and our first kiss on the beach of Cádiz. Her lips pushed into mine for one hot moment. Then she was gone. I imagine Angelica's nights in Sevilla. She must have slept like this with the luxurious linen and the sweet smell of soap. Her wealthy patron and lover, Augustine, curled around her. I had no chance. I wish I had understood then, understood the lure of luxury. I had been too cruel with her. Life had been too cruel with her.

I fall asleep like this, like a baby, tangled up in fabric. I rest long past dawn without the cries of heaven's barking jackals. But then I am awakened by sounds in the other room.

"We have to have it for tonight, Mark. Tonight. We have a full house, I can't risk it. It has to be there. Also double-check the chains that will lock me in the bottle."

My eyes pop open. The room is filled with a sunlight: so blonde and brilliant! It almost makes me cry. It has been so long since I have seen the Earth's morning sun. I float down the halls to see her, her hands moving in tense circles as she speak,

"Tonight is the debut," she paces. "That's what they're paying money to see. The bottle has to be ready."

"We're worried about the sealed flap—it's not holding well," the young man says to her.

"Strap it down, just strap it down better."

"It's going to make it harder for you to get out."

"Then finish it this afternoon, so we can do a run-through," she stands close to him, so he can see every line in her face. "Get it done by 2."

***

The same girl who is so pale and sad in sleep stands like a beauty sparkling beneath a row of lights. Jeannie walks down the center of the stage, her palms on her hips, in a tight red dress with long black stockinged legs and a top hat. How many days did I strain just to see an inch of Angelica's legs, hungering at the ankles for her knees? My eyes trace the slender line of thigh from hip to toe and look over at Saint Michael. He smiles with an impish grin and pats my knee, "Show time again!"

"Ladies and gentlemen," announces the girl with the blonde hair, her breasts squeezed into a sequined dress. "The Ingenious Jeannie Price, the death defying diva."

A ring of flames explodes around the magician, her hands lift into the air.

"Tonight Jeannie debuts Jeannie in a Bottle—her latest escape—and you will be the first to see it—and hopefully, not the last. I am Sandra Bandara, your MC tonight, and get ready to enter Jeannie's Magic World . . ."

Children sit with apple cheeks besides their parents, their mouths open, the flames in their eyes. Men sit with their lovers, hands clasped, waiting to be fooled. Yes, to be fools!

"Your first magic show, Carlos!" Saint Michael pats my arm and grins again. I smile weakly. I can't imagine why tricks would mean more than truth. It was the same in Sevilla with the gypsy dancers and the new guitars. All for a good show! But who wanted to hear the laments of a lost soul without money, food, or love who spoke the soul's secrets and the dark truths of a gypsy? "Give us the alegrías," they would say! "We don't want those mournful gypsy songs." But those were the only kind I sang, for all life gave me was a moaning throat. The cante jondo, the deep song, almost found its grave because of those good shows, with their pretty girls and handsome boys who strummed. Those were the days when it all began to change and flamenco was stolen from us, from my people.

"Carlos," Saint Michael points, "can you do that?"

The girl on stage juggles long swords. The glittering edges spin as they twist in the air. She catches each sword at its handle; I imagine her hand gripping the blade, the sting of error. The tension delights me, like watching the great male gypsy dancers whose feet were too fast for the eye, who could take away the breath!

"Me? " I shake my head.

"Let's see you, " Saint Michael pushes me down the aisle. "Go, go, juggle with the girl..."

"What?"

"On stage, great cantaor, show her what you can do with your hands."

"I'm an Angel of Death," I bite at the air. "I cannot touch the material world. You know that!"

"I used to juggle in the circuses in Africa."

"Africa?" My forehead wrinkles in disbelief. "Circuses? What are you talking about?"

"Do you dare, Carlos?"

"How? What?"

Saint Michael throws an imaginary sword and then another and another. "Imagine hands full of love and a heart of pity for the girl. Teach her a lesson in magic—but with kindness, Carlos Peña. Can you do that?"

To touch again! To feel a glass of wine, a knife, a loaf of bread! I look down at my hands and feel the electric light of life. Saint Michael winks.

"Imagine you juggle the heart of Piedro. Imagine you catch his tears in your palms. Imagine the grief of a child who lived without him. Know you can touch again. Go!"

I run up to the stage and look at the faces before me. I am invisible, but I feel the force of their eyes. The room shrinks and grows with one huge breath; we angels have our powers, but the living have the wind of life. The sighs of a thousand people come my way, in and out, like one big breathing animal.

***

The first time I notice the smooth skin of a girl is when I meet Angelica: the girl who stole oranges from the friars' orchard when I was just a boy living in the Home of the Poor.

Several days after I first saw her, I hear a scurrying. I think at first it's a mouse seeking its morning crumbs. But I listen again. It is coming from outside. I go to the stacks of crates with tomatoes, near where morning's bread cools on long tables. The girl, the girl is there. She is reaching for a tomato.

"You can't do that," I say, grabbing her wrist. "Drop it." I want her to pay attention to me. I know that I have power over her now. It's one way to keep her near me. I like the feel of my hand on her, my skin against skin.

She holds onto the tomato until I squeeze with the strength of my palms. She tries to pull her wrist from my hand, but I won't let her. She has the thin skin of a gypsy; I can see her bones. My hands have the meat of a well-fed boy now.

"Let go," I say.

It is the girl I saw climbing the trees nights before. I can tell by the thick mane of hair and her small body. She does not look afraid, and I like her strength. She refuses to surrender the tomato.

She has a determined chin and strong forehead. I have never seen anyone who looks like her. She has a head full of curly hair, wild, not tied back in ribbon like most gypsy girls of my day. And I have never seen so many curls on one head. She has eyes that are green, and I wonder if she is part payo. Who has ever seen a gypsy girl with green eyes? Maybe, like me, she has been exiled from all who should love her.

"You're stealing," I say, but I like her. So I loosen my hand.

"I am hungry," she pouts.

"Okay. Okay," I say. "There's cheese in the icebox. I can get you some." The boys are still singing upstairs, so I know we have time.

"You will?" Her eyes brighten.

"But we have to hurry. Morning mass is almost done. Stay here. Shhh..."

I know why the gypsy children pluck and steal bread. My belly is full in these halls, but I remember the days when I was always hungry. I sneak over to the icebox, and open it as quietly and quickly as I can. I reach up for the cheese, wrapped in paper, always in the same place. That is how I know where it is. The letters Q-U-E-S-O are written in black, but I cannot read them. I know the world by where things are placed not by the words attached to them.

"Here," I say, running back outside, my heart beating with joy. "What's your name?"

"Angelica," she rips through the paper and stuffs cheese in her mouth.

"Not now. They might see you," I say. "Hide it."

She presses the package into the waistband of her skirt

and pulls her shirt over it.

"Do you live near here?" I ask.

"Sort of." She has bare feet beneath the hanging skirt, and her hands are strong with all the signs of a girl who has worked since she could walk. I am thirsty for the beauty of dark skin, for the skin that is mine, the skin with all the depth of a million songs. They are in her. I can tell. She looks at me with eyes that do not turn away, unusual for a girl.

We hear the whistle of Father Ference, and Angelica dashes for the bushes. I want to grab her and keep her with me. Instead I turn around and see his large frame.

"What are you doing outside, Carlos?" Father says.

"Nothing, Father."

"Where's Francisco?" he asks.

"He's inside, sir."

"I thought I heard voices out here." His eyes are tired. If there is a God, he does not dwell in the heart and mind of Father Ference. The God I believe in climbs the wall in the flames of my fires.

"Come upstairs now for morning prayers," he says.

"Yes, Father," I say.

Angelica is lost somewhere to the orchards. I want to say goodbye, but I must walk like a dog at Father's side. On my knees, I imagine her again. Prayer is a good time to dream and plan naughty deeds. I am already eight and she must be the same age as I. Dear God, I say, I hope Angelica comes back to find me. I look up while the others are quietly praying. I imagine I see the girl with curls on the roof. She is dancing round and round in a dress of white linen with a long tail of fabric. She is dancing and saying my name... Carlitos.

Soon Angelica comes in all my dreams. Where once fire was the savior of my pain, she appears in a white dress, spinning in circles and laughing. I think of riding horses down the streets of Cádiz, galloping along the beach with tall ships sailing out to foreign lands in the waves before us. I dream of Angelica dancing around campfires while I sing to her as my grandfather did to La Cicatriz. I ache again for gypsy songs and long nights of summer sky.

***

I wait and wait for her. I check the windows every night, and in the mornings when I hear scurrying, I look for her. I look for the girl with dark curls. Months pass, and I begin to think that I never saw her. She was only a dream, a ghost, like my mother who was there, but then gone. Gone.

We boys rarely leave the walls of the orphanage. A secret cloud hangs around the monks. We are told that they do their work against the wishes of the government. I do not understand, but I know that this is a forbidden world here, forbidden and isolated.

The good boys can go out to do errands. They are dressed in pants and shirts like ordinary Spaniards and are sent out into the day to buy pencils, polish for leather, stamps from el correo. But I have not seen the streets for so long. I would do anything to roam them freely. I imagine I am with the girl walking the promenade with its market and stealing lemons and oranges. But she does not come.

I give up any hope of seeing her, and hunger again for fire. After lunch one day while the other boys go back to classes, I tell Francisco I must find soap for the dishes. I escape upstairs past the chapel to the attic.

I carefully close the door behind me and get out the matches and kindling I once hid in the drawers of an old dresser. The beams hang low in this room crowded with old and broken chairs and tables. It is full of a promising wood, wood that could make flames that would break out beyond the roof into the sky above. It would be my biggest fire yet. I am no longer satisfied with the small burns in sinks or garbage cans. With time, it takes a larger fire to appease the sad heart, the hunger for death. I will set the blaze in the very back of the attic, so I can get out without harm. I never imagine that the flames will devour me. They are like the warm arms of a loving mother and a father who would have fought for me, all in the spire of the flame. I set the kindling in the back near broken chairs and then—

I hear footsteps and the creak of an opening door. I turn from the kindling and look at him. It is the teenage Lorenzo, with his officious air, the one who carries the rules in his pocket and tells me what to do.

But he has no right.

I hide in a corner crowded with chairs. "I knew it was you," Brother Lorenzo says, coming towards me.

"Too late to hide now, Carlos. I knew you were the one… and I found you. I came prepared." He carries a pail full of sand.

"Where's Carlos?" everyone asks. He taunts me now with a voice that is mocking and cruel.

"Where could he be? I knew where you were. Setting another of your fires, right?" He pours the sand onto the struggling flames. "I've been watching you all day—you are pretty clever, Carlos, but not as smart as you think." The sand suffocates all of my beautiful flames. "There now. Who should give you your beating: Father Ference or me?" He comes after me crouched in the dust. "Would you like a beating in front of everyone—or just here, the two of us, in our cozy attic? Come here, Carlos. Let's get it over with."

He has taken my only power from me.

He gets on his hands and knees and grabs at me.

"I could just lock you in here, you know. Or will you listen to me and do what I say? Come on, take off your clothes and we can get this over with."

"I don't want to take off my clothes," I say.

"Have it your way. Take off your pants," he says.

"No," I say.

"You need to take your punishment. Or should I just

report this to Father?"

"No, don't," I say, gulping down my words, crawling out from under the tangle of wooden legs.

"Get on your knees," he says. "I need to spank you."

I pull off my pants.

"Your underwear too."

Lorenzo stands there. At first I feel a painful whip of his hand, but it is only his hand, and I am used to pain under the hateful touch of Flora. But then his arms are around me, and he pushes me towards the floor. I turn around to look in terror as he flattens me face down. His arms pin my shoulders. His penis bulges against my ass.

I try to break free from him but he tightens his grip. "Calm down," Brother Lorenzo says, thrusting his hips against me. He puts his hand over my mouth. My teeth try to tear at his palm but cannot. He forces himself into me with all the weight of the world, and I feel I will split in two. My face is frozen in a grimace, with the heat of hate. He grasps at my hair. I try to lift my face from the floor, but as my head bobs up, he pushes it down.

I twist and turn trying to break away, and catch a glimpse of his face. His eyes close, his mouth is slack, like a baby's. Then he shudders. My torn flesh screams even more. A moment later he takes a deep breath, then stands quickly. The heel of his shoe keeps my mouth pressed into the floor, so I cannot get up.

"Clean up the mess." He kicks me, then releases his foot, tossing a rag down to me. I roll over and pull up my pants, my ass aching and his juice staining the backs of my thighs.

He walks out. My jaws clench with the closing door. I rest on my side, looking out at the white walls, the smell of newly killed fire in the air still. The flames inside the hidden forest, the place where the trees are small, collect in the ember of quiet. The heat rises.

That night I dream about the erections of priests and the sad eyes of nuns. I dream about Angelica and that brown hand taking tomatoes. I say, "Give me a bite, let me have that." My hand touches my body in the secret of the dark. I imagine igniting all beds of the boys into flame, watching their bodies twist in the pain of heat. I dream about fighting my way out of a house full of fire. I am standing there out of breath, there is smoke coming out of my mouth.

Two days later in the early morning, the baker has retired early into the chapel. I hear steps. They belong to her. I am certain of it. My heart quickens. My God has heard my prayers. She stands at the back door with her wild hair, lit by the sun, her black eyes hungry and sad.

"Angelica!" I say. I will make her happy with more food. I will fill her belly with the true sacrament. While upstairs they sing the praises of a good God, we worship the breads and the cheeses.

"Hi," she says. Although her face is sad, she tries to lift

her mouth into a smile.

"Hi." I try to find courage in me to ask, but I am not sure how.

"I have more food for you."

"Where?" She looks inside the kitchen without any fear. She does not know that I could be beaten for my good deeds. This is how it is here. Charity is not for all. She watches as I pull cheese from the icebox and grab a small bread.

"Here," I tie the bundle of cheese and loaf into a cloth towel.

"Thanks."

There is a long silence, but I cannot let her go easily this time. I must ask her. "Can I come home with you?"

"Home with me?" she says, as I give her a small piece of yesterday's bread. "My father wouldn't like that."

"It's horrible here. Please."

"But you have food, shoes, everything here."

"I need to get out, please."

Her eyes scrutinize me. She looks at my feet in brown shoes, and my brown pants and then my long arms. Then she looks at my pleading face. I pour all I know of love and goodness into my begging voice.

"Please, Angelica."

"But he might get angry," she says, biting into the bread. I do not know then, but it will be this way our whole lives. I will plead, and she will say yes, but only almost. It is never a yes entirely. It is always, always with hesitation... until I lose her. But now she is the key to my freedom. I will give her everything I have, anything she wants.

"Please. I'll do anything."

"Okay," she says. Crumbs cling to her lips and she smiles. It is a smile I will love my whole life. It comes rarely, but it is sweet.

This is a girl who is serious and strong. Only sometimes the sun cracks through her dark skin, but when it does, it is more than light, it is everything in Cádiz, everything in Spain, everything there is.

7.
ESCAPE ARTIST

Toitos le piden a Dios
La salud y la libertad;
Y yo pido la muerte
Y no me la quiere dar.

Everyone asks God
For freedom and good health,
I, however, ask for death
But this He will not grant me.

Five long minutes pass. The people fidget in their seats but say nothing. Even Sandra is without words. They are focused on a metal container shaped like a bottle and locked with the magician inside. Sand runs through a large hourglass beside it.

"If she's not out in 20 seconds," Mark whispers to Greg. "We have to do something...there's a latch in the back of the bottle, but you bring the axe for effect—distract them while I take care of it..."

This is the talent of the magician: crouching towards

her grave in a water-filled vessel. Hah! How many times can she escape death, just so that others can sit there and watch, waiting, waiting?

"Should I do something?" I turn to Saint Michael. We stand near the timepiece, close to the blonde-haired girl, her eyes aimed at the unopened jug, no signs of the magician.

"Go find her, but let her go to the edge of death. This time you must not save her."

I float towards her, but just as I do, Jeannie appears, eyes bloodshot, hair falling around her eyes. The audience gasps and then breaks into wild applause.

Saint Michael squeals in delight, "Marvelous!"

"She's done it again!" Sandra sings into the microphone. "Death-defying Jeannie Price!"

Jeannie raises a chain and lock above her head in victory. Then there is a puff of smoke, and the girl is gone again.

"How'd she do that?" I ask Saint Michael.

He leads me backstage to a wooden labyrinth of stairs and slides below. "Down there... trap doors."

I look to see the girl storming up several stairs as she heads for the young man, Mark. "Are you trying to kill me?" She throws the chain onto a table. Even though I have no body, I step away in fear of the girl's wrath. "The seal. I could barely get out of it."

"You said," Mark follows her to the catwalk. "You said

to tighten it. So I did."

"You're a liability," she says. "You're fired."

She trots up metal stairs onto a bridge above and makes her final entrance to the roar of applause. The black bathing suit clings to the girl's damp body. Wet and sparkling, Jeannie Price emerges from the tomb... again.

When the applause ends, she climbs back down into the world of crates and boxes and the theatre begins to empty. Behind the curtain, the magic ends; whatever is left of it lives in the minds of those who were once seated there.

"You okay?" Sandra rushes to the magician's side.

"Mark fucked up the seal...but I survived," Jeannie smiles with the smugness of a girl who has escaped death.

Her eyes are big. Conquering death gives her the illusion that she needs no one. I can see it. I recognize it. Carlos Peña was careless too in his days as a gypsy. Oh, my magic was another thing altogether, but it was the same cruel stare. I overcame the petty deeds of men. I could work until sunrise without food, outwit the priests and even Angelica. I could live without sleep, food, love. My cool heart never needed, just wanted.

Carlos Peña once chased death, and Jeannie Price tries to escape it. Each of us with our swollen heads thinking we are bigger than all this! Hah! In the center of that power is the weak sad boy, Carlos with memories of a bed of dirt where the flies buzzed against his ear. I look at the girl with her tough tight jaw and wonder, what does she escape, really? Whose grave calls her?

"Hey Greg! Could I catch a ride with you tonight?" she squeezes his shoulder. "I've got a great bottle of vintage cabernet at home. Let's celebrate another death defying escape. You were great- by the way," she says, "The perfect magician's assistant..."

***

"Look at these LPs! Charlie Parker . . . The Happy Bird. And it's signed. You know what's this worth? Where did you get these?"

"My dad," Jeannie points to a photo of a bearded man on the wall. "He had connections."

"Connections?"

"My dad was Rick Price—the jazz musician. "

"Rick Price? Your dad?"

"Yeah."

"I have all his records. Every one," Greg says. "I collect."

"You do?" Jeannie asks.

"The man was a genius."

"Genius. Yes, Rick was." Jeannie points to the box. "Why don't you just take those? I have no use for them anymore."

Greg pauses in disbelief. "These are worth thousands. You sure you don't want to keep them for yourself?"

"I got duplicates of most everything. Just take them."

"Wow Jeannie, thanks. Ah... whatever happened to your dad? I never knew the whole story."

"He was murdered. Right in front of me and my mother."

"He was murdered. Oh... I'm so sorry...There were so many rumors back then... It was hard to separate fact from fiction..."

"My mom did all she could to keep it hush... hush... there were so many secrets... just so many things she would never talk about."

Greg puts the record down. "That's horrible."

"I learned to cope."

"What an awful thing—How old were you?"

"Twelve."

"Young. That's terrible."

"Yup. The big secret."

"And now your life is about escaping from bottles?"

"You mean like I have an obsession," she smiles and gulps down the last of the wine. Well, Dr. Freud, it's a theory, right?" she stretches her arms up like a cat. "This time, I win— not death. Not some asshole with a gun. I escape, so dad can escape. Besides I've always liked attention, the spotlight, you know. I didn't have my dad's talent for music, so I started pulling rabbits out of hats. I did that way before the shooting. It's a rush, like adrenaline..."

"Aren't you afraid you're going to someday push too

far?"

"No. I'm not stupid... but I got to be careful who works for me. Damn Mark." She shakes her head as she reaches into the box. "Here, you like flamenco? Take some of these too. I could never really understand this music. "

"Carmen Amaya." Greg pauses. There is a photo of the gypsy standing with her hands curled over her ears. Her hair is tied back with a red flower, and she wears pants. A bailaora without a tail of fabric behind her? She dances in the straight legs of a man. Imagine it!

"She was the first woman to zapotear in the twenties," Greg says.

"Zapotear? What's that?" Jeannie asks.

"The footwork, using the toe and heel, like tapping. Used to be only the men did it—and the women used hands, arms, the upper body."

Whoever she was, Amaya was not the first. Angelica was. She wore no pants, but she danced with the fire and intensity of a man, drilling her feet onto the stage. They all whispered about her then, that she was neither man nor woman when she danced, but had the grace of a girl and the passion of a man desiring her. Piedro, Piedro, I think as I watch the American, you knew my Angelica, didn't you, in the days she lived with Augustine, when we were apart?

I look down at the floor with grief. What would his guitar have sounded like playing to my songs, the sad wails of

The Orphan, El Huérfano? Would he have tapped the guitar's hollow body as I howled my cantes? In those days I did not trust the guitar. It was new to flamenco.

Song was the core of gypsy music—all else merely surrounded it. Gypsies clapped their hands, rapped their knuckles, tapped the dry sticks for rhythm. The gypsy singers would rock the gut with words, but when the payos discovered flamenco, they did not care for the mournful songs of a wailing gypsy. "Bring out the dancing gypsy girls! Let's hear that pretty guitar!" the tourists would say. But the guitar was just an echo of the true instrument, the instrument of my God, the God of voice, deep song of life's suffering. I stare at Greg's hands. Was it he who met me on that hill at dawn and died by my hands? Eh, Piedro?

"Do you have a LP player? I'd love to play this one."

"Yup, I do. Nothing's like vinyl. Over here... "

No cantaor of my day could imagine such a thing: engraving one's voice on a disc, so it could live forever, going round and round. Could that still be flamenco really? A cantaor gives everything he has to music, singing all night, knowing dawn will come and the throat will have nothing left, and that the song that he has sung is gone forever.

A gypsy's voice trembles through the empty rooms of mosques, into the courtyards of old señoras with their blue pots and wrought iron tables. I hear the voice of every man in the music, and I am not afraid to say so. I hear the ghosts of tortured Jews and Moors lamenting to Allah. I hear the weeping of a man who has lost all his children in the gypsy slums of Andalucia's Triana.

> *Como pajarillo triste*
> *de rama en rama saltando*
> *asi está mi corazon*
> *el día en que no te hallo.*

> *My heart*
> *is like a sad bird*
> *jumping from branch to branch*
> *the day I don't see you.*

Spanish men, plump with bread and wine, would listen with their whole bodies, waiting for the note that would make them wail, for a flamenco cantaor is measured by how well he breaks open the heart.

They said in my day that Carlos Peña, El Huérfano, sings with the wildness of a dog, a howling dog, that El Huérfano can make all the world feel the sadness of being alone. But I was young and my voice was not like the great singers, whose words are stretched in the back of the throat, resonating in the chapel of the skull, as does the voice of the man I hear on this spinning black disc.

"Flamenco is about emotion," Greg says. "Depth of

emotion." He understands the heart of my gypsy music.

"Not really pretty is it?" Jeannie brushes her hair back with the edge of her hand. "But powerful." She leans back into a chair and lets her eyelids shut as the voice washes over her.

"Flamenco isn't meant to be pretty. It is meant to moves us." He takes a sip from his wine. "What matters is the soul, duende, the passion of the singer. Singing and dancing is like... Like being possessed completely by feeling... by spirit."

"Want more wine?" she stands up and heads to her kitchen.

She returns placing the chalice on the table. Then Greg takes her hand in his and stands beside her. "Here, maybe we can get duende moving through us." He pulls her toward him. "Listen to that voice, can you believe it? Listen. Does that do anything to you? Does it make you want to move?"

She looks down at his hand as it touches hers, and it seems to calm her, the presence of his skin, the weight of bone and flesh.

"Yes." She lifts her hand into the air, loosening his from hers, teasing him with her rolling hips. That's it, Jeannie, I say. "I think I feel it...the duende," she whispers into Greg's throat.

She straightens her spine, her fingers curled. The veil of her hands passes across Greg's face. They are moving like sea current, back and forth in gentle swells. They join where the shore hits the waves, the very core where life is made.

Go, I say. Go with him. Let yourself fall into his arms.

He will catch you. And I will bring you dance. A dance you will never abandon.

"Are you afraid?" she asks, her mouth against his throat.

"Afraid? No. Why?" Greg pulls at her.

"I haven't danced since I was a girl. I stopped dancing years ago. Just stopped."

Jeannie stands, her hands bowed above her head. She taps her feet and spins in a circle, brushing her hair back with her hands.

"¡Olé!" I cry as she spins. My leg stiffens with the rhythm of a solea and I clap and sing. Tell me that you love me, that you believe in me, brown girl of my soul, tell me, tell me now. Her hands rotate around her head.

She lets out a sigh and stares up at the ceiling with the open gaze of a child in wonder, as if there are stars there. "Did you hear something?" she asks

Jeannie, who are you, sweet dancer? In this moment, this girl has the power and beauty of a woman who is not afraid of spirit. The great dancers and lovers surrender themselves to life. She stands with strong squared shoulders, her small ass tucked beneath her. I imagine her clothes falling away. Where will his lips fall first? I think of his tongue following the path of her veins, and the moist wet heat of her center where life is made and sweetened. I imagine her hips widening to love.

Yes, love is better than death.

My legs squeeze in the memory of desire. Will Angelica

find me one day in heaven, the sun streaming through that wild hair? Is this Angelica before me in the body of a magician? Jeannie spins one more time, then pauses to look at Greg.

This is a dance that is older than the vines and keeps blooming. It is in the soles of Angelica, in the gypsy toes of dark-skinned señoritas as well as señoras plump with aging bellies. This dance has no year, no day. The dance comes through with the same green force of life for all who invite it. Flamenco will not die, and it is in her, the magician.

"Put on more music," she says. "Let's dance to more gypsy songs."

Imagine sitting in a Spanish plaza, dipping your fingers into the pools of water. See yourself in the reflection, imagine him, looking at you in a rippled surface which also holds the memories of the Alhambra illuminated in the light of a full moon—with your love wrapped around you, and your kisses damp as the cascading fountains.

You will love Greg, but it is not him, just as the dance is not yours, whoever she may be, whoever you once were.

Come with me, Jeannie, just now, come.

You will find love here. And I, Carlos Peña may someday be a muse, may someday give death away forever.

8.
ANGELICA

Tienes los ojiyos grandes
Como pieras e Molino,
Y parten los corasones
Como graniyos e trigo.

What large eyes you have,
As big as millstones,
And they grind up hearts
Like so many grains of wheat.

"Let's hurry!" I say, pushing her toward the stone wall. And she does. I follow Angelica down roads I have never known, first through the narrow alleys, balconies filled with flowers, sweeping brooms and whistling men. The world is all mine. I am free! I wander the winding dark veins of stone streets, run far from the hymns of the boys.

"I think we're safe now," I slow to a walk. "Besides, the friars never go out."

"Why?"

"They're not supposed to. They could get in trouble."

"Trouble?'

"The church doesn't like them."

"Oh," Angelica says, not truly understanding, and neither do I. But as we talk, I note the path where we walk because I have already decided. I am not stupid. I have dreamed so many times of it, and I will make it come true. I will return at night with balls of kerosene and let them explode at Lorenzo's feet. Angelica's breath slows as her lungs fill with air. She does not know that as I stand there I am thinking of it all, making a map in my head of the road where we stand.

"What's your name?" she looks down at her feet, catching her breath.

"Carlos," I say. "Carlos Peña."

"Peña." She says my name and then searches my body with questioning eyes.

"Your mom and dad are dead?"

"Yes," I say. It's mostly truth.

We walk until we come to a plaza. There is a white-washed church with a golden dome. Pigeons fill the steps below it, and there is the smell of café and fresh pan, bread. Angelica has no shoes. I am lucky. Mine are worn and ugly, but they keep my toes protected. Dark-skinned men and fair women pass by. Here one can see anything. Even the sea. The ocean is huge, like the vast fields of Jérez but with a swelling blue power. Waves come to the sand, lapping one after another, then leaving behind white foam as they dissolve into the pebbles. Tiny fishing boats are tugged in, tugged out, tugged in with the gentle current. It is as if I was born here.

"I've only seen it once— when they brought me here." I take in a breath of salt air and look at the gypsy girl. She stares at me in surprise.

"Only once? Didn't they ever let you out?"

"No." I think of all the world I have not seen, of how many waves have come to shore as I sat behind those dark walls.

"That's awful." Angelica's green eyes have a gray cast now. The wind makes a wild black halo of her hair.

***

The image dims on the lunar table. Saint Michael turns on his light.

"She still amazes me," I say. "She was like Patia—both were such wise girls."

"Yes, God sent them to you, but... well, they were angels who were sent but also taken from you. Unlucky life."

"Is that what it was? Unlucky?"

"That's one way to see it. The other, of course, is that it was a lifetime of soul ripening. The hardest lives are like that. They ripen us. Like your time in the House of the Poor. There was much to learn there, but you chose death instead, Carlos. Your bad luck then became your evil," Saint Michael says.

"What?"

"The last fire. You took two lives, Carlos, and several

were hurt."

"Two lives? There was only one. The old friar."

"No," Saint Michael says. "Two. Brother Juan, the baker, was the second. And many more injured. Would you like to see the scarred faces of the boys?"

"Brother Juan?" I say with a sinking heart remembering the kind baker.

"You may want to forget," he says like a strong father. "But I cannot let you."

"It's terrible, Saint Michael. But I had my reasons. You saw what Lorenzo did. He had no right. No one had the right."

"But you did? You had the right? There's a world of difference between what we feel and what we do. Understand, Carlos?"

I sit up. "I know the difference. But I did things for a reason." I look to the door of the Palace of the Muses. What would happen if I were to run out and never return? More long days of bringing the dead home, back to the barking jackals.

"Reasons?" he says. "Good lives are not made of reasons."

"I did what I could, Saint Michael." I know what he says is true, but Carlos Peña was just a boy.

"You did. But will you do better next time?"

***

Angelica takes me to the crowded barrio of Santa Maria where the gypsies live. It smells of bad sewers. Homes are crowded with the barks of children, dogs and roosters. She tells me music is played all night in the café cantantes all around the gypsy quarter. She points to one and tells me, "That's where my father sings, and I dance there." The narrow streets carry the sounds of clapping hands, singing and sometimes guitars. It is not the music sung to angels but songs of love that is broken. The hymns of the boys are lost to the clouds; gypsy songs come into the human heart and fill the jaws with life.

Angelica lives in a lemon-colored tenement packed with voices and faces, but I am not ready to live there. "I'll be back tomorrow," I tell her. I roam, from café to café where even a boy can sit in the back and watch the cantaores with their droaning sad voices and the beautiful women dancing to their words. I wander the streets. I press my face into the windows of bakeries with their sugary treats. I pass the stores of watchmakers and tailors. Long dresses of every color hang in shop windows.

As I walk into an empty alley with its crooked stones, I think again of Lorenzo. All this time, the streets were breathing with life while I was forced to live by rules made for a God I did not believe in. Perhaps I should feel the gratitude of a freed slave, but instead, I feel the bitterness of revenge. I think of boys ridiculing me, of the monks who made me face the wall and say my letters while the others laughed. I think of Father Ference's heavy feet and how he would stand above me with that thick tongue, of Lorenzo's body slamming me into the floor with the bludgeon of his penis.

I fall asleep in an alley. It is still night when I awake from dreams of fire, high blazes with screaming faces rising from them. The streets are dimly lit with hanging lanterns. I look up and smell the rich sea-damp air as I shiver from cold. I step inside a café cantante and see an old man singing, his forehead crunching with the high notes. Two girls, almost my age, are dancing on the darkly-lit stage. The heat of song, and smoke, warms me. Men and women, their half-filled glasses crowding the small tables, tap out flamenco rhythms. On one of the back tables I spy a bowl brimming with matches and two empty wine bottles. I slip the matches into my shoes and sneak away with the bottles, one in each hand. Outside again, I follow the map in my head, remembering the wall near the sea and the domed church. I retrace my steps to the Home for the Poor. I follow the roads as they twist and turn with their high buildings leading to plazas and fountains in the dark. Then I recognize the street where the stone wall meets the curb.

I climb over the high wall quietly. When I hit the ground, I stay frozen for a moment until I am sure no one has heard me. I go to the kerosene. They have hidden it many times from me, but I have always found it. It is where it was last left, behind the pile of wood in an unlocked box. The shutters of the cottage are open, which is what I had hoped. One spark from the kerosene-filled bottles will set the wooden beds and their coarse sheets blazing. I have heard everything burns hotter in a stone room. Fire will devour what it can; its appetite is without compassion.

I take off my shirt. The ripping of the seams crackles in the quiet air, but I move quickly. Then I think I hear steps, so I drop to the ground and freeze. When it is quiet again, I take one piece of my shirt, stuff it into the bottle and then pour kerosene. I pull the matches from my shoe. I throw a lit match into the first bottle. It catches. I feel my beating, frightened heart and a tense joy as I stare into the glow of oil. Then I rise, run a few steps and heave the bottle into the monks' cottage. Shattering. I quickly climb the wall again. I hear frightened voices. Erupting flames entice me, and I want to stay to watch, but I know I must run or be caught. I jump to the ground on the other side of the wall and escape. Good night, Lorenzo, I think. Imagine a lover with a wick for a tongue, its mouth enveloping you. Imagine your ass burning, deep within its core, like the cruel sting of you inside me.

***

"And so the fire burned. Yes, Carlos, it did," Saint Michael says.

"Yes," I say.

"Father Ference and his brothers lived in secrecy since the Catholic Church opposed their sect. Did you know that?"

I shake my head.

"So they could do nothing although they knew it was you. They knew you set that fire, but they couldn't go to the authorities. You got away with murder," Saint Michael says. "Devout monks who practiced their charity underground . . ."

"I was lucky, then."

"Lucky? Luck is getting away with harming others?" Saint Michael shakes his head sternly. "It would have been lucky if you had been punished, so you would have hurt no one else. Lucky, Carlos? Better you were locked away from the rest of the world, so you would not have killed again."

"I was not that evil," I say, standing up. "I was not."

"What is your idea of evil, then, Carlos?"

"I didn't mean to." I step away from the chair, eyeing the way out, my feet pointed at the door. "Lorenzo raped me."

"But Lorenzo escaped unharmed while innocent men were killed. What did you mean to do?" Saint Michael asks.

"I was raped, treated like a dog there."

"You had a full belly, a warm bed."

"What kind of God lets rapists escape without punishment? You tell me St. Michael... "

"And then?" Saint Michael says, "You left behind a trail of ash and death. You were careless."

"No, not always," I say, tears building in me. "I had some mercy."

"Mercy? What mercy for the two who died in their beds? Don't you think it's time you look and face what you did?"

"I had a reason. I wanted revenge." My legs weaken.

"Does the world revolve on what Carlos Peña wants?"

"No, Saint Michael," I say, lowering my head. "But why did they get to have what they wanted. Why them and not me?"

"God judges all fairly, Carlos Peña. Lorenzo is not immune from karma. He has his price to pay-understand?" The room darkens again as I stand fearfully watching the lunar table. Screaming men rush for a door that is stuck, that will not open. Fists bang against the wood as flames devour the beds and sheets. Voices cry out in shrill desperation. "Let us out!" The lunar table dims, and I hear steps. I feel a presence near me. I look up, and in the dim light, I see Brother Juan, his face blistered and scarred, brown and red, with seeping wounds where the fire ate through the layers of skin. His eyes are deformed, no longer the shape of olives, but melted half-closed. His lipless mouth opens.

"Carlos, Peña..." he says all energy drained of him. "I said no boy is all bad. I said I would watch you in the morning. I told Father Ference that I had faith in you. I saw the spark of goodness in you. I saw it. Why then, Carlitos? For all my work? Do you know the years I spent to make that orphanage? How many years of prayer and labor, so we could take in young boys like you who had no home? Why, Carlos Peña? See what became of my hands? Skin all burned off," he says breathlessly.

"No!" I fall to my knees. "I didn't mean harm, really, I just meant to save my dignity."

"Dignity?" Brother Juan asks. "Dignity? For this?"

The monk looks down at me with his charred face. There are flames reaching into the night, burning on the lunar table. The yellow glow fills the room. There is the breath of the flames, the heavy demanding breath of fire. Then there is silence and the white glow of the imageless lunar table as the ghost disappears into the ceiling. Saint Michael reaches his hand to his scraggly beard and lets it rest there.

"You murdered, Carlos. You took away life. You had no right."

"Forgive me." Each tear stings my ethereal skin. I look into my cracked palms and feel the horrible pain of living in a body that's been eaten by flame. A century without feeling, and I have forgotten the intensity of Earthly pain.

"There is nothing wrong with raging against injustice. What Lorenzo did was wrong, and you should have been angry. But killing must never be a choice for you again."

My silence tells him that I know. There are no words for a truly sorry heart. St. Michael walks close to the glowing sphere and looks at me in compassion.

Then he points. "Angelica."

She stands with her hands above her head, her hair, her, brown chin tilted slightly, her feet sunk into Earth.

"She was a dancer from the beginning, wasn't she?" he says. "Come on, get up, off the floor, now." He motions with his hands.

"Yes," I say catching my breath between tears, rising to my feet again. "She was. Yes, Angelica was."

9.
CANTAOR

Mi llanto a nadie conmueve,
Cantando paso la via,
Mi llanto a nadie conmueve,
Yo soy como el ave fria
Que canta al die de la nieve,
Al amanacer el dia.

My tears move no one
And so I sing my life away;
My tears move no one
So, like the little bird
Shivering at the snowline,
I mark the break of my day with song.

"Who was Jeannie?" I ask Saint Michael. We are seated in our velvet chairs with the doves calling behind us in the Palace of the Muses.

Saint Michael smiles with affection. "It's a puzzle—isn't it?"

"Angelica?"

"No, not Angelica, but you already knew that, Carlos. Jeannie was a girl you never met, a part of your life but no one you knew, really."

"Was she Patia?" I am sitting now on the edge of my chair, my hands tightened on its arms.

"Carlos, Carlos." The great angel laughs at my impatience. "It will all be answered. Sit back. Now, how were things on Earth?"

"I think she senses me, feels me, feels the first hints of duende."

"That's marvelous! I thought it would take much longer. So she's returning to her natural gift." Saint Michael strokes his wispy beard.

"Natural gift?"

"She could see and feel the muse once, had the gift of the threshold, but like so many, she shut the portal door and with it, of course, duende died."

I look out at the doves in the gilded cage and my mind drifts to Greg.

"Are there always traces from the past when people return to a new life?"

Saint Michael smiles. "For some there are hints, and for some there are none. Women who were great dancers may come back as invalids the next life. It all depends on the lessons that need to be learned. There are no hard and fast answers. The more you find out, the more complicated it becomes. The small mind cuts the world up into easy sections, like an orange." He turns to his fruit bowl and hands me a tangerine.

"Thanks," I say.

"It's good practice." Saint Michael winks. "Try it. Look!" The lunar table brightens.

There is Juana, Angelica's grandmother. Her body is plump, and she wears an old blue dress without sleeves so that her flabby arms can stay cool. Her hair is pulled into a long braid on her head.

"I won't sing for money," she is saying. "I sing because it is in my soul. But it hurts to sing. Miguel tells me I will rip my throat, but when I hear other people singing, and it is no good, then the song comes from my gut, and it wants to burst out, and I cannot keep my mouth from opening."

Juana sits on the stoop with four other gypsies in the shadow of the tenement in Cádiz. One is her husband, Miguel, who is much older than she and already blind. Also there is Lauro, Angelica's oldest brother, who is dark and lean and almost a man. Angelica's younger brother, Pablo, and sister, Maria, sit beside him.

Although late, it is summer, so the sky is still light. The streets are filled with the orange of a setting sun. Piss-filled water drips near the well in the courtyard behind the open tenement door. The building is full of cracked surfaces. It is as old as it is dirty. There are chattering voices inside.

I approach Juana.

"Does Angelica live here?" I have traveled through the streets to find her again, have walked since dawn for the Home of the Poor, since I have lit that raging fire. I hope they cannot see through me to the naughty deed.

"Angelica? What do you want with her?" Juana says.

"She told me to meet her here."

Her brothers and sisters are staring at me.

Juana turns to the window. "Angelica, someone is here for you." She stops at the open door and waves.

"Bring the boy a shirt," Juana says to Angelica. She slips back inside to get it for me.

I have forgotten that life is bad for gypsies and for a moment I want to run back to the Home for the Poor where the walls and floors are clean and there is a line of shiny basins. I catch sight of a woman in a skirt that hangs with dust; her three children packed into the small foyer of the tenement. Angelica's father, Luis, pushes past the children to the stoop. He is small and thin as if life has narrowed his shoulders. One lock of white hair flops over his eye.

"What do you want, boy?" This man has many worries, I can see, and getting enough food for his family is one of them.

"I am an orphan, sir," I say, hoping for pity, looking towards Angelica to help me. But there are so many orphans these days, so many gypsy children without mothers.

"He was the one at the hospicio where I got food." She steps near me, handing me a worn white top. "He's the one who gave me bread and cheese, papa."

"Oh," Luis says. "What do you want with me, with my family?"

"The brothers didn't like me. I didn't belong there, sir," I say.

"At least you had food and a good bed there. We don't have much. We can't feed you," he says.

"I am strong and clever. I can get food." I show him my hands that are small but have long fingers and the dirt-veined skin that is proof of hard work.

He looks me up and down. "Well, you can stay for a week, then I'll decide. What is your family name?"

"Peña. I am Carlos Peña."

"You must earn your keep here, Carlos. We will be heading soon to Jérez for the harvest and we will see how hard you can work. We'll see." He shakes his head unhappily as he slips back into the shade of the house.

Angelica pulls my arm and leads me in a dash down the cobblestoned streets. They are narrow and uneven, but I am like a horse that has found its stride. We run for blocks, and I look around at the line of shops and old homes with balconies that have cracked corners or missing rods. There are women looking from their balconies, children tugging at their hems. Homes are crowded with gypsy families. Rivulets of filth and human waste overflow onto the streets. The smell of urine is everywhere as are the sounds of coughing. Behind closed doors death takes children, fathers and mothers. But I am still a child myself, and these things do not concern me. I follow Angelica gleefully through the streets to the ocean.

I run down the beach with her, taking off my shoes. Sand sprays my ankles. "Here's my favorite place," she points to a long stone pier that stretches far into the sea. "Let's go!"

We run down the pier. At the end sits an old castle, the brown walls sunk into the waves. When we get halfway, we stop to look down into the swirl of blue water.

"You know, my mom is dead too," Angelica says. "She got a sickness."

"Oh." Such facts do not startle me. She walks ahead, turns, and then claps her hands. She smiles, framed by the pier and sea and the castle with its mountain of crumbling stones. "Do you want to see me dance? Give me some rhythm."

It has been three years since I have sung gypsy music, but somehow my body remembers a melody. I give it my own words. "*I knew a girl who danced near the sea,*" and I sing and start clapping. I watch Angelica's pink toes and brown feet, the calluses and curling toes pressing into the hard stones of the pier. Angelica has heels like rock, toughened by walking on gravel and dirt, toughened by poverty.

"I am surefooted," she tells me. "I always keep my balance."

As she dances, the whole sky fills with the purples and pinks of twilight. Her back arches and she lifts her arms above her head as if she holds the pica, the javelin that flies into the belly of a bull. She is like a matador with arms coiled back. Her hands strike the air. "Race you!"

We rush down the pier, over the sand, onto cobbled roads. I look through iron bars into kitchens packed with families cooking, the smells of garlic and old meat, anything that can be eaten. Later that night, music explodes in the hands, feet, voices and guitars. We rush outside to the courtyard with its waterless fountain, which is chipped and broken, and its dirty well. We sit on old chairs and wooden boxes. Angelica dances while Lauro sings and the others clap.

What kind of bird is that
Singing in the olive tree?
Go tell it to be still
Its song makes me so sad!

Angelica's small arms are like serpents around her head with the slithering grace that seduces and also soothes; the spell encircles her. She is named the snake, La Culebra, and when she is older, her whole body will move as if it has no bones. But that night she is a child of nine years. As I watch her dance, I recognize the look of possession in her face. This was what I felt when I entered my secret forest, when the flames rose from my matches, and I heard the song of a fire. I watch La Culebra as her arms twist towards the sky. I especially love to watch her move when her eyes close. It is like I am home when I see her face.

Luis, El Relojero, begins a tapping rhythm with a dry stick, palo seco, on a small wobbling table beside him. El Relojero, the watchmaker, glows with the birth of song. It is almost like the sweaty sheen of a man after having made love, but it is also like the brow of a woman laboring before birth. It is the song gaining its power.

"That's it, yes!" the others urge, rapping knuckles, nodillos, to bring rhythm to his song.

El Relojero closes his eyes as he descends into an unknown dark.

Money in your pocket—

His fingers claw at his shirt, he tugs at the fabric, as the veins in his neck release the song.

—maybe should be guarded,

Sweat forms above Luis's brow, on his throat, his chest.

But the we—al—th of the he—art . . .

Is lost if kept to onese—lf.

This is not merely singing; it is widening the whole body, so the spirit enters. The song weighs upon flesh as does the sun on the back of a father who digs a grave for his child in the summer heat . El Relojero opens his eyes and looks around him as if he has traveled far and finally returned to the land he loves.

"Singing is more sport than art," Luis says wiping his head with a clean ragged handkerchief.

"I was sick twice from duende," Juana tells her son. "The body could not take it. You must be strong to sing." She speaks with a gravely throat.

I can feel the strength of it now, feel how pain can be the agent of song. I have pain in me, I know. I have songs that wait inside.

"Can you sing, Carlos?" Juana asks.

"Me?"

"Yes," Luis says. "Let's see if you really are a Peña, for they can sing, The Peñas . . . Sing for us, huérfano."

"Eso, that's it," says Lauro. "Let's hear what the orphan can do." He pulls a borrowed guitar close to him. I look in wonder, for I have never seen a gypsy play guitar.

Juana laughs. "All of us end up without mothers and fathers when we are old. We are all born to be orphans! God's cruel trick! Sing, boy, sing for all us orphans."

I am nine years old, but I know the song is in me. This is not the lighthearted tune of a boy singing to his new friend on the pier, but the kind of song that calls from deeper places, cante jondo, that comes from a person's soul, not the throat. My own voice forces itself through my teeth as if it is someone else's.

Ay Ay Ay.
I was born an orphan
Whose mother's life ended
When I took my first breath.

The song has its own life, and the tail of this animal is thrashing in my gut. I do not even see the others watching, but I hear their sticks and the clapping hands, the palmas and jaleo of strangers.

"Eso es, chico!" I open my eyes to see a circle of faces, all looking at me, and Angelica with a bright smile has her hands high in the air. I am hot. My neck feels like I have swallowed coals.

"You can sing," Luis says.

"He's a cantaor! El Huérfano!" Juana claps.

In the years to come, I will sing the songs and Angelica will dance. I will sing to her about mothers who are ghosts—so thin and ugly that they frighten their own children—about the sweet taste of oranges and the bitter taste of death. And I will spend my days singing of a heart that is abandoned, of a child who seeks its mother. We are only children, Angelica and I, but we have found our passion in the gypsy rhythms of flamenco. We are the orphan and the snake.

When Angelica is eleven, she starts dancing at the café cantantes, the ones that have opened on Cadíz de Marques, and we are there all night with Luis, Lauro, Miguel, Juana and the others whose names I have forgotten. The cafés are crowded with gypsies and tables of wine and olives, not yet with tourists and their new gypsy shows. The music we make is real gypsy music. Every night, El Relojero invites me, "Sing a sad orphan song." There are nights Angelica dances until dawn and then until noon when the others have gone home to sleep. Luis worries that she is possessed by demons; others see angels around her and bring her their jewelry. She is young, but she has it, we all know she has it.

"Take this money to La Tejedora," Juana tells me, pressing the bills into my hand. "And keep your eye on the woman. Make sure she doesn't ruin Angelica's good sense." La Tejedora, the weaver, is well known for her careful, colorful steps woven together like a great tapestry when she dances. But she is also known for her loose morals. "They talk," Juana whispers to me as we stand in the kitchen alone. "And it's true. I've seen her myself with the payos in the saloons. But she dances like no one else. She'll teach your sister."

La Tejedora is one of the best dancers in Cádiz, if not in all the region.

"If you want to dance, think of nothing else," she tells Angelica as we walk into the courtyard of her small stucco house. Doves sit on a tiled bench surrounded by jasmine. Beside it are six cobalt pots overflowing with pink geranium. La Tejedora has a long face the color of warm cinnamon and a mouth the shape and color of plums. Her eyes are sorrowful, but her plump legs are filled with grace and power. La Tejedora's long black hair is pulled into a tight bun. She plucks a crimson trumpet flower off the vine and slips it behind her ear. "Okay, let me see you now. Can you sing for us, Carlos? An alegria."

I sing the first refrain. The teacher and her new pupil are clapping.

Come with me
Come with me
Tell your mother
I am your cousin.

Angelica dances with open hands and an arched back. As she moves, she draws her hair up into a knot on her head.

"Stop," says La Tejedora. "How can we dance an alegría without a bata de cola?" The bata de cola is the bountiful train of the dancer's dress that is used like a thread woven between the legs and waist, woven like a spell as a woman dances.

"I don't have a dress for dancing," Angelica says. The fabric is expensive, and she is still young.

"Come, come with me," Teje says. "I have something for you."

We follow her into the cool house with its smooth walls, no cracks or buckling wood. There are plants and rose-filled shawls, mantillas, hanging from the wall. She has photos of dancers framed in painted wood with their names signed in black. She opens an armoire to reveal hangers filled with flowing dresses. Angelica's mouth widens, her hands reach to the fabric.

"They're just dresses," La Teje says, smiling at Angelica's wide eyes. Even my eyes grow big seeing so much wealth in a gypsy's home.

"I wish I had these." Angelica steps closer as if she wants to climb in and sleep in them.

"Maybe you will," Teje says. "But not too soon. A girl must ripen first. Fruit picked too early will never sweeten."

As early as then, I can sense two different desires. These dresses mean nothing to me. All a singer needs is one pair of pants and one white shirt. The song has no frills. It is only now, in these days, that there is more: the dresses, the guitar. They are all the new flamenco.

To me, the material world does not matter. As long as I can eat and be free. Where there are things beyond my skin, there is always the risk of pain. To me the things outside mean nothing. The life that matters is the one inside. But Angelica is a girl and dance means the full ruffle of a dress sliding across her ankle as she slips into it.

La Tejedora hands her a dress. "Here, red is your color. We will need to shorten the hem and arms."

She takes Angelica into another room to dress. I whistle to myself. I am a boy of twelve, and Angelica is eleven. We are brother and sister, or so they call us, but this is beginning to change as our bodies change; the seasons are turning us into people we would not be otherwise.

"What do you think?" Teje says as Angelica stands before me in the full red dress.

The dress is too big in the shoulders and too long at the hemline, but Angelica stands proudly as it falls around her hips and legs. She is more than Angelica now; she is a true bailora, a dancer—what she always has been—but the full hemline makes her a woman, one who can fan the heat of warm faces.

"The train is too long, but this will be good practice." La Tejedora leads us outside to a row of stones.

"Move the dress side to side as you step, and do not let even one thread touch the rocks, understand? And keep that head up. No pierdas la elegancía. Do not lose your elegance."

Angelica dances over the stones, shifting the dress from side to side and behind her, so the hemline does not touch the ground.

"Good. Let's practice with a partner. Imagine I am the man. Good, now I come zapoteando, tapping my heels and my soles. Now our dance begins. One, two, three, one . . ."

La Tejedora approaches Angelica with her arms straight out from her sides and her hands in fists. She clicks her shoes on the ground in an intense rhythm and stomps on the earth with the strength of a man.

"How do you do that?" Angelica asks, her head tipped

to one side.

"I study men. A woman can't dance without knowing how a man moves."

Angelica's eyes look up where the trumpet vine begins at the corner of the roof. Her mind is busy.

"I would like to dance like a man," she says. "On stage."

"On stage? No, no," La Tejedora laughs. She looks at Angelica and strokes her hair. "These steps are just for our practice, dear. We are women. Zapotea is for the men."

Later as we walk home, Angelica turns to me. "I am just as strong and just as quick as a man. I want to dance like one. I want to dance, zapoteando." She holds the dress close to her. My eyebrows raise, and a laugh escapes. Angelica is a rebel like me. I hope life never tames her. Still I reply, "Dance like a man? But no girl does that."

"La Culebra does." She cracks that small smile that grows slowly out of that dark and serious mouth, with her chin and jaw leading her face, with her brown-skinned pride.

10.
ZAPOTEANDO

Pensamiento—aonde me llevas
Que no te pueo seguir?
No me metas en caminos
Que yo no puea salir.

My thoughts—are you taking me
Somewhere I cannot follow?
Don't lead me down paths
I can't find my way out of!

Almost a year later, we are at the Café Del Oro. Angelica is in her long red dress, with its ruffled layers, along with black-heeled shoes that were a gift from La Tejedora. El Relojero sits at the foot of the stage and invites me to take my turn. Lauro sits next to me with a guitar, borrowed from a payo in Sevilla. I sing a solea, which draws upon the grief inside me. This is what I sing best. Alegrías are for anyone. The grief of a solea is for Carlos Peña.

Mother dear to my soul

How I love her
I will always carry her
Deep in my heart.

When my words are done, Angelica comes to the stage as she always does for the prelude before Enrique joins her. She looks out at the audience, her black hair in a braid, her head perched in determination. La Culebra is known for her gentle slithering arms that rise up out of the fire of her belly, but this time instead she throws her arms out to her sides and curls her hands into two fists. Angelica lets loose rapid, drilling steps, pulling her skirt up, so her feet move freely. The audience sighs in surprise, for Angelica, this twelve-year-old girl with small new breasts, is dancing like a man, tapping heels and soles, stomping the floor.

"She's dancing like a man," the women whisper, and the men lean forward to watch when they see her power and precision. But they never leave, despite how much they gossip, for there is something Angelica possesses that everyone wants.

Her cousin, Enrique, enters the stage. He looks confused, but he advances toward her as he always does, and she just dances faster, thrilling the audience with the tension of her steps. I look at her with stunned eyes. She glares back with a powerful joy.

Angelica circles Enrique with the flirting grace of a girl, but her feet move with the rapid, sharp strokes of a man upon the stage. Her green eyes have no thought in them, and the small moustache above her lip gives her this peculiar beauty, so that she is neither sex. Heaven above, Earth below, Angelica is afraid of neither, her head held up high, her chin squared in concentration, her fingers curled above her skull.

I look over at Luis. He sits as if he sees nothing although his daughter stands there like a man with brave and unrelenting steps. He sips his wine. He put his hand to his brown throat. There is both fear and thrill in his face.

After her dance, Luis waits for her at the side of the small raised stage. He leads her to a table in the back as the others watch her. She is young and daring and is possessed by spirit.

"You are not a child anymore," he says angrily. He squeezes her arm and pulls her into the chair beside him. "Dancing like a man is a child's game. You are a woman. It's time you live like a woman. I want you to marry." Angelica reaches for an olive and sips her father's wine. His hands hold back an impulse to hit her.

She has shown disrespect for the traditional ways. Her brow is covered in sweat, lips red with his drink. But he knows that she is La Culebra with a face that everyone loves. Not even her own father can strike her without being scorned.

***

"It happened to me too," La Tejedora says, sipping sherry. "It's time to marry," they told me. "But I said I wasn't interested. They insulted me and gossiped. I didn't care. Dance always came first." Angelica listens as she tightens the buckle on her shoes. "News spread about your dancing last week, Angelica. Zapoteando? What a brave wild girl you are, but don't think for a moment that men's dancing is better than ours. Now let's practice with the dress. Men use their feet, we have power in the hemline."

La Tejedora stands behind Angelica and grabs hold of the dress and gathers the fabric in her fingers. "Do you feel this movement?" Angelica dances while La Tejedora guides her across the courtyard.

"You are a born dancer," La Tejedora says embracing Angelica. "Is your brother still playing guitar?"

"He says he will play and study in Sevilla." Angelica sits on the bench, pulling her dress away from her ankles as she lets them be warmed by the sun.

"That's good. The guitar is everywhere now." La Tejedora stands behind Angelica, braiding her hair.

"No instrument is better than singing," I say. The voice comes from God. The rest is man-made.

"No?" says Teje. "So, you're a purist, Carlos. But change is good for an art form."

"Guitars belong to the payos," I say. I am so young, but I carry the worries of the grandfathers. "The voice is all gypsy."

"Flamenco belongs to gypsies and payos now. This is good for the music." She wraps white ribbon at the end of

Angelica's hair.

I look at La Tejedora cruelly. She is surprised. She knows the Carlos who is kind and mournful, not the one who once set flames to the beds of children and monks. She turns from me. I have never meant that much to her.

"We have to live the way we want to." She comes to sit beside Angelica. "You are born to dance, Angelica—husbands and children are too much trouble." These words both please and worry Angelica, but she listens because La Tejedora is her idol, the woman who has become what Angelica wishes to be. Teje has no family, but a house full of dresses and mantillas and the pictures of the famous. "Marriage is good for some girls," Teje says. "Not us."

As for me, I will never marry. There is no question about that. I will always wander and wait. Just wait for Angelica. For the day she will know, know the truth that we are meant for each other. And I will never steal her from dance. She will dance to my songs when I am an old man with no eyes left. I am certain.

A year later in summer, we sit outside. Juana tells me so the others can hear, "Each cantaor has his own brand of suffering. This is what makes you sing so well, Carlos. You are not afraid to suffer."

Lauro sits on the stoop and stretches his legs onto the street. "Suffering does not sell. They come to hear happy songs, see beautiful gypsy women. In Sevilla, they are giving away money to gypsies who can put on a good show."

"A good show?" I say. "They steal our music. It's payo greed." I am fifteen, and I speak and think like a man.

"I could use some of that payo greed in my back pocket." Lauro stands to show me the hole in his worn pants. "You're just a boy, Carlos, you don't understand. The money is just waiting."

Angelica looks curious, but I look at her disapprovingly.

"You should come to Sevilla," Lauro says to Angelica. "They love a pretty gypsy dancer."

"There's more to it," I add. "The payos get rich on the backs of our pretty girls."

"Who says? Besides, what do we have to lose? This good life?" Lauro points behind us at the crumbling tenement.

Juana sits like a mountain, then sighs. "The cantaor is the center of flamenco. When Carlos sings, it is the ghost of his mother. Her ghost finds comfort in his throat. Can a guitar do that?"

Lauro shakes his head. "I like my guitar. It is good for our music. Ghosts or no ghosts."

"Guitar and pretty costumes for the girls," Juana snaps and closes her eyes. "Real flamenco turns the guts out. It refuses to hide behind the mask of beauty."

"I'm leaving in the morning for Sevilla," Lauro says sharply. "There's money there for a gypsy who can play guitar to a full house. I am not afraid of wealth."

Angelica turns to me, so her grandmother cannot hear. "I don't want to have children like my mother and then get too weak and old and die young. I want to dance on stage and be rich."

The music is not for money, I think. It is a longing. It is a mother whose life is taken for no reason. It is my own dark face and the sour taste of a mouth whose stomach is hungry. Music is what keeps us alive; it is the force that never doubts itself; it is God standing near the riverbank and offering oranges as Carlos falls onto his knees begging mercy.

But to Angelica, music is something different. It means new shoes and long dresses. I say nothing, but I know. There is a wide river forming between us, and it is larger than the Guadalquivir. She takes my arm in hers. "Let's walk," she whispers. I follow her. I always do.

I look at her flowering body. I have thoughts that betray hers. But they are only thoughts. I imagine her naked lying by the sea. Her nipples are beautiful and brown, and I suck them. Wetness is everywhere: in the black lace of her, on her thighs, in her hair, everywhere. I grow hard. But she feels nothing for me but a sister's love.

She looks into my wandering eyes. "What are you thinking about?"

"You in Sevilla."

"What do you think?" she asks.

"You'll be rich someday."

"And you'll be there too?"

"No. I don't think so." I shake my head, "I'm staying here where the music is not for sale and I am not owned or sold."

***

It is spring and the vines are flowering. La Tejedora stands next to Angelica who is poised with her arms out, her feet pointed, her hair in a wild mane. "One two, one two, then back." La Teje moves with the quickness and instinct of an animal.

"Angel!" It is Lauro. He is the only one who calls her this way. I hate the name. She is no angel, but a girl with dark muscle and tough skin. Earth is her heaven: her spine, mouth, dancing feet.

"I'm back from Sevilla." He walks into Teje's courtyard and plants a kiss on Angelica's cheek. His generous head of hair falls above his black eyes and long lashes. He is handsome. Even the Spanish girls laugh shyly when they pass him.

Teje's face brightens. "Hey, Lauro, you brought your guitar. You can play for us." She has always liked him more than me. Most people do. He is handsome and musical and daring. The others know my songs, but few know me. I am Angelica's confidante. This is my real fame. My songs bring tears to some, but I do not have the boldness that makes for greatness, and I do not want it. I'm not a handsome boy. And I do not have the glimmer of ambition. But Lauro does. He

154

smells of good fortune.

"No one in Sevilla dances better than you, Angelica." He leans upon his guitar, his pelvis pressing into the neck of it.

"She is good," La Tejedora says. "But it's one thing to dance because you love it—and another to do it for money."

Lauro laughs, the yellow of his teeth showing. "Look," he pulls out a handful of pesetas. "Easy money."

La Tejedora puts her arm around Angelica's shoulder. "I won't let her out into the world until she is ready."

"She's still learning," I say.

"I can speak for myself, Carlitos." Angelica looks right at me with lips that almost pout but remain strong with that unrelenting jaw.

Lauro tells us about Piedro, a man he has met who plays guitar like an angel. "It's the best guitar you will ever hear. He makes any singer sound good. Come back there with me."

I will not go to Sevilla. And I will not let her go.

"She's not ready," I say. "La Tejedora knows. It's not time." I look towards the great dancer, my eyes begging for her to agree. I feel I own Angelica, and she senses this. She looks at me, and pulls away. She says nothing but her body speaks for her. I see the hatred in her eyes for me, and I wish I could change it to love.

"I am old enough now. I can go." Angelica says. A spring breeze lifts her hair from her face.

"Angelica knows herself. If she feels ready, she should

go." She takes a strand of Angelica's hair and wraps it in her fingers with love—almost desire.

Angelica looks at Teje and then at me. Her eyes seem to calculate distances, remember kind touches. A wave of doubt crowds her face. I know her well. She must go with someone she trusts. Not Lauro. Me.

"Maybe I'm not ready yet." She puts her arm around La Tejedora. "But soon."

Lauro kisses her forehead. "If you change your mind, I'm going by train in the morning."

"Train?" Angelica's eyes brighten. Most gypsies do not ride by train—at least not with a ticket in their hand.

When Lauro has gone, La Tejedora puts her arm around the girl, "You have to go some time."

Angelica rests her head on her teacher's shoulder. They are like mother and child, like sea line and shore. And I am as I always am, the lone cantaor with a song that cries out even when it is not heard.

***

"You are the only one who understands," she says to me. "Even Lauro thinks I should marry soon. He says lots of dancers are married."

We are walking near the pier. Lauro is in Sevilla again. It is autumn. The season of harvest. The fruit that was blooming in spring is ready now to be plucked. Angelica is ripe, looking more a woman than ever. She is as tall as I am. Her strong body is full of curves. Her eyes are less green and more the gray of waves at dawn before the sun fully rises. She has begun to wear her hair in a bun with ribbons, pulled back to show her face, but by the end of each day, a few stray strands escape from their binding, and spring out wildly around her face. It makes her beautiful to me. Not beautiful like flowers but striking like the side of an impossibly steep mountain.

We are like brother and sister, but we are not, for we also know the tension of our differences. We look and smell differently, come from a different nest, and while I vowed I would never touch her, there is always the pull of her that sinks its gravity into me, like the sea where we walk, like the tow of wave to wave. I have spent much of my boyhood sleeping next to her, feeling the sweet curve of her arm against me and sometimes pushing her to the wall, so the small bed is mine. She is family but she is not. Familiar and unfamiliar in the same body.

"They think all girls should marry," I say.

She looks at me. Her gray-green eyes invite me, and to this day, I do not understand what that glance meant. What was she asking me to do? To fill her with life and make her big like the other girls? Was she daring me to steal her dreams from her? One day she hates me for wanting to possess her too much and the next she wishes to be loved and possessed.

"Carlos," she says. "I want a kiss. Just one." She closes her eyes and her lips, plump and reddish brown, open slightly.

"But we're family." I know the words won't matter. Words rarely do with her.

"But we're not, really. Besides, you're the only one I trust. And I want to know what a kiss is like. I am fifteen now. It is time."

I am drawn into her lips and kiss her with a power I had never known was in me. I fall in love with the power as much as I do with the sweetness of her lips. My mouth still pressed to hers, I open my eyes to see her, and I feel queasy. This is my sister, Angelica. But she's not. I am ashamed. And I am hot. I feel her lips widen as mine pull further apart to receive her. My heart races. I look in her eyes and I see what I have always looked for in the eyes of women. But I am also ashamed. It is like starting fires in the Home for the Poor: forbidden heat under the roof where I live. I pull back from her.

"That's nice." Angelica's tongue sweeps her lips.

I am worried someone will see us, so I pull her into the shadow of the bluff.

"Will you kiss me more?" she asks.

"Yes," I press her again to me.

Her cheeks are flush, with the heat of a woman, and her breath is faster, inviting me to give her more. "That's good," she says.

"How about this?" I say, gently pinching her nipple through her blouse, pulling her to me. "Is this good?"

"Maybe," she says purring, opening her arms, and I

know she is mine. I rub my hands on her belly. And with all the weight to my body, I push her down into the sand, pressing her mouth with my tongue, my pelvis into hers.

Suddenly, she sits up as if from a dream, awake and horrified and throws me off of her with all her strength. She stares at me for one long moment as I get to my feet. Her hand is pressed against her lips in shame, and she then wipes it against the skirt as if she is cleaning me off of her. Without a word, she dashes away as she did the first time I saw her in the orchard at the Home for the Poor: black hair tossing behind her—ghost, animal, smoke.

I walk to the shoreline and dip my hand into the sea. My body stiffens in shame. I wipe cool water onto my cheeks and walk back into the heat of noon, following the footprints Angelica left into town.

11.
SAND

Es to queré come er viento
Y er mío como la piedra
Que no tiene movimiento.

Your love is like the wind
And mine like a stone
That never moves.

Saint Michael pulls his shoes off and dips his feet into sand. "Brings back memories of childhood. How about you, Carlos?'

"Yes, of course, of Angela and Cádiz."

"The sea is everything to me. Being fully realized is wonderful. Someday you'll be that way too, Carlos, living in both worlds, one foot in the mortal world and the other in the ethereal—"

"Oh," I force my toes into the sand, feeling nothing. Jeannie and Greg approach, walking hand in hand near the sea. Saint Michael runs ahead to join them, and I follow along, slowly, battling the wind.

"I love it here. Been so busy," Jeannie follows Greg to the edge of the roaring surf, "... no time for ocean walks."

The waves are wild, more wicked than those of the bay in Cádiz where fishing boats drifted between catches.

"Too much working," he shakes his head. "We're all working too much."

"Come here, Carlos," Saint Michael pulls me to his side. "Greg, Jeannie—all of us— are like grains of sand."

I understand.

Molecules are rearranged by breezes, but the soul remains unmoved, like the bed of the sea. Above, the waves and winds change form, never the same, no permanent shape, but below, on the ocean floor, all is constant. The face is new, but the soul lies far below in stillness

"Look at the scar, just like Piedro's... and those hands," Saint Michael whispers.

"What?"

"Shhhh... Not now..." Saint Michael presses his finger against my lips. "Yes, even as we change form, some things remain the same."

Sandpipers scatter as Jeannie and Greg walk near, footprints swallowed by the foam.

"When do we need to get back?" Greg pauses.

"Rehearsal's at 2."

Their heels move together, one, two, three on the beach, picking up speed, then slowing in rhythm.

SAND

"Hmmm..." Her eyes follow whirlpools of sand as she heads for a driftwood log and sits there, reaching for Greg's hand. "Here, come next to me."

Saint Michael leans against the log and motions me near.

"Remember when you were a kid, and you'd bury your friends at the beach?" The girl I could not kill looks out in the waves, gaze drifting.

"Yeah--"

"Wouldn't that be a great idea for a new escape... sink a casket into the sand... bury me alive..." She turns to him, wind blowing her hair into a veil across her face.

"Don't you think?"

"Bury you alive?"

"Yes. I like that. Very theatrical... and everyone can relate to it... days at the beach... childhood... but taken a step further..."

"Another new way to escape death?"

"Yes--"

"You're obsessed." He puts his hands onto her knee.

"Yes, and what's wrong with being obsessed?"

"Well, you're obsessed with death."

"I'm not." She turns toward the sea. "I am obsessed with defying it!" she smiles broadly. "I used to do kids' birthday parties, you know, fifteen dollars an hour, but pulling rabbits just didn't do it. You want to be successful? You have to think

163

big, drama—bigger than birthday party tricks. Everyone wants to triumph over death..."

"You mean YOU want to triumph over death—"

"What does that mean?"

"Your father..."

"No, no. You don't know me. Don't psychoanalyze me, please. "

I know I must have known them both in my other life, but they returned to Earth years before me, obviously. I was busy bringing the dead home while they were riding bicycles and taking walks in the park with their families. But who were they?

"Hey... you can't tell me that the way he died didn't affect you..."

"Well... my dad... had a big... no, a *huge* ego. Remember the accident? How you and everyone said it was a miracle— that... I barely had a scratch— I say I don't believe, but there's this part of me... I like the idea that my father's spirit came back to save me that day. Yes, that was a nice thought that he was there, watching over me, caring for me...."

Jeannie wiggles her toes in the sand, and I come behind her, resting my hands on her shoulders. From this other side, we have affinities with souls on earth. We do not always know why or who they were in other lives with us. We are drawn to them from the heavens, drawn to land like moths on their lampshades.

SAND

I am a stranger to the 21st Century and as much a stranger to this Jeannie Price, the illusionist; she is a shallow picture to me, a pale faced girl. Her skin is as white as any payo's, and I do not understand the mysteries of her soulless life. But there is in her brown eyes the depth of desire, I see it. She is longing for me, for the songs of a cantaor, for a dance that is buried beneath her pretty fragile face, that longing that lies beneath the magic tricks. The longing that binds me to her in some way.

"The other night you told me you had not danced since you were a girl...

"When I was a girl, I used to love to dance... for hours to my father's piano playing... Last night when you talked about duende, I thought of it..."

"You were a dancer, then?"

"Not really. I went to ballet classes and hated them. It was like the dance they taught me was different than the dance I felt inside. And when I was 7, I had a recital. Dad came with one of his girlfriends and the usual entourage, and mom as usual just sadly tagged along. The whole thing was so sick. Dad was the big star, so everyone played on his terms. And the music begins—classical music—and we start dancing, but I hear something completely different."

"Like what?" Greg turns to face the girl.

"My own music, beautiful music. I closed my eyes and was carried away by it. While the other girls were dancing one way, I was in a corner, spinning and twirling in my own world." She laughs, "I was completely in my own world—completely out of step with the others."

Yes, yes, I whisper. You heard the muses from the other side. They must have loved you once for dancing their music. Loved you for inviting them in. Like Angelica.

"I felt this incredible happiness," Jeannie's face softens, "and then my ballet teacher dragged me off stage. 'You have no respect for dance!' she yelled. My father stood beside her. 'Are you trying to shame us? What the hell is wrong with you?'"

"But you were just a kid... and you were full of imagination... like kids are..."

"But for my dad, appearances were everything. That night when I came home, he slapped me across my face told me I had no respect for him or for music. That was the last of dancing lessons... and dancing for me."

"He crushed your spirit."

"Well, not all of it, just my dancing spirit. "

In Jérez I was tied to the bark of a tree for stealing a few grapes from a brimming basket. What crime is it when a child wants the sweet wine of life, who hears the muses hum, who yearns to dance to the music of the blood... who aches for the lulling nectar of a mother's love?

"Where was your mother during all of this?" Greg asks.

"Around, but she was a weak person. Dad had these girlfriends who took up most of his time. She felt like she just had to live with it. After all, he was a genius, right? The great Rick Price," Jeannie rolls her eyes. "When there is that much talent, the world revolves around you... That was life with father... the world revolved around him..."

"And you've made a name for yourself too, Jeannie..."

"Guess so with this bag of tricks."

"You have found your own art."

"I like to think of it that way. Now... what about you... what's your art, your passion?"

"Right now," Greg turns to her. His tender hand reaches for her cheek. "It's you."

"Don't get too attached," Jeannie says. "Please."

"I won't," he says, holding her chin in his hand and then meeting his lips with hers. I wish I were human again and could feel the salt in my teeth, the hot mouth of love. Jeannie's eyes close, as they fill with a hint of her soul. Her chin has softened. I open my mouth and imagine what it must be to feel a kiss again. Kiss. Jeannie reaches for his neck, lost in the delicious honey of him. And I—almost jealous—gaze away, towards my home, far beyond the clouds to the executioner's quarters.

"Mmm," Jeannie says with the full blush of love. "Let's just go slowly. One step at a time."

Jeannie and Greg walk arm in arm near the restless sea. The waves and Carlos Peña are witness.

"Ahh... maybe this will work out, after all," Saint

Michael puts his arm around me to draw me near. "When we are human, pieces of our soul are stolen from us. The muse's job is to bring those pieces back."

Greg and Jeannie walk, and with each new step, leave a trail behind them as impermanent as the footprints that Angelica left for me, marking a path through the pebbled roads of Cadiz.

***

In the Café Del Oro in Cádiz, Augustine's white skin shines like the edge of an egg. He is too clean, too full of money. I see violence in his face immediately. The others tell me they do not recognize this in him; they see a man who is well-groomed and shrewd. He comes here from Sevilla, looking for gypsy dancers and musicians.

Flamenco is more popular than ever with the payos and their friends in Sevilla. The ones with money bring gypsies to their businesses, homes and parlors, to sing and dance our souls. The rich get fatter while we barely have our dimes, barely have homes we can live in.

Yes, a few gypsy stars live well. That's the hope of La Culebra, my Angelica. But what is the price of a gypsy's soul?

Augustine, the payo, stands in the back of the café. His hands are in his pockets. His fingers stroke the grooves of his coins as he watches Angelica. He looks with the intensity of a cat as the bird leaves its nest. I watch like the dog in the neighbor's yard barking. La Culebra's hips pull the cat towards them with a dizzy slow roll. The cat licks his chops.

Angelica dances tonight to the songs of El Escondido, the hidden one, and his family. Later, when dawn approaches, I will be asked to sing a solea. But only when night is deep and the most profound, music is made. Now they play the early music, and although it is gypsy, it is lighter-hearted than the music of the hours when most have gone home to rest their drunken throats.

At the end of the third song, Augustine walks up to the stage and turns around so everyone can see and hear him.

"La Culebra can dance—eh?" he says. "But let's see how well she can. I have one thousand pesetas here for her." He holds them, so all can see the fan of bills in his fat palm. "If she can dance over thirty sherry glasses without spilling one drop."

Women lean into their lover's ear and whisper, "One thousand pesetas!" It is a year's worth of wages, even more for a gypsy. My stomach turns. But Angelica smiles at him, smiles with the edge of desire. One thousand pesetas could buy dresses and shoes for a lifetime.

"Is the bet on?" He comes close to her, waving the bills in front of her face. "What will you give me if you lose?"

"I won't lose," she says with a large grin. "But if I do, you can have my firstborn child." She throws her hands in the air. It is all show. I know this, and I admire her. Carlos Peña could never stand so boldly.

Augustine calls to the café owner who comes to the

stage and sets down the glasses and sherry. Chalice after chalice stands there, narrow and long-stemmed, until there are thirty. Angelica approaches. She has practiced for hours with the rocks in La Tejedora's garden, but even I am afraid that the train of her dress is too big for her.

Augustine points to the singer on stage, El Escondido, to pour sherry into each one. "To the rim," Augustine says. As El Escondido pours, Augustine motions for the audience to repeat after him, "One glass, two, three . . ."

The room fills with smoke, with the anticipation of the dare. I suck on an olive pit. Some spectacle, I think. This is a man who knows how to put on a show, like the organ grinders whose monkeys come with their tarnished cups to beg for coins. In all this time, Angelica has not looked at me once. Augustine has filled the room like three suns as golden and white as summer straw. She is blinded by him. I am small and dark, like the splinter of wood that no one sees but gets under the skin.

"Ready?" he asks her.

She closes her eyes for a moment, inviting duende into her. She looks out at the line of glasses, each brimming in sherry. The guitarist fans his fingers across the strings. Beside him an old woman claps palmas claras. Then the cantaor begins:

Que el sentido me quitas cuando te veo en la calle

SAND

I can't think straight when I see you on the street.

Angelica snaps her wrist towards the earth, and then gathers the folds of the long dress into her hands. She turns her back to the crowd, raises her arms, and then spins around with eyes open and fiery like a bull's as her nostrils flare. She stomps, head up, her hands on the hemline, side to side, with measured steps across the glasses. Her dress snags the rim of one of the chalices, and it topples. But she then steps back, the fabric guiding the teetering glass into place, no fallen sherry. She tugs at the fabric again so that her knees and ankles are showing. Her jaw tenses, sweat gathers on her lips. She fans the frill of her skirt above the last few glasses. Twenty-two, twenty-three... She glances down every few steps but never behind her. Twenty-nine, tap, tap, thirty. She stomps her soles into the floor, lifting her knees high. She uncurls her hands above her head in triumph. ¡Olé!

Augustine claps. "¡Olé! La Culebra," he says. The audience cries out for her. "Eso, chica!"

Augustine hands her a folded bill. "Hold this in your teeth while you dance. The rest waits for you in my pocket after the show."

Afterwards, she finds him. He looks at her. His eyes go to her full breasts. "The money. Under one condition. You come with me to Sevilla."

"What? But you did not say that," she says.

He shakes his head as if he is a boy and does not know the rules of life. "I did not know until I saw you dance over those glasses. Now how could I resist you?"

"She won that money." I stand close to him. I am at least ten years younger, but I do not care. I have been beaten by bullies before. I have little fear left. "Give it to her now. She does not have to go with you."

"Who's this?" Augustine asks as if I am invisible.

"My brother." Her words sound kind. She does not say my name. I am now as I have always been, the one who remains nameless.

"She won that money," I say again firmly.

"Come to Sevilla with me," he whispers. "You will be a star." He is short with wide shoulders. His mouth softens with a vulnerability I do not trust, but Angelica sees something tender in him. He holds his hands out to hers, his palms so soft because they have lived on the sweat of others. How could she ever say yes? He promises her two hundred pesetas per month, and he will give her a room with a soft bed and heat in the winter.

"All you have to do is do what you love," he says. "Just dance for us, four nights a week, maybe a Saturday afternoon."

She looks at me. She knows I do not like this man, but she also knows I love her and want her to have the things that most dancers dream of—at least warmth on cold nights, and the chance for the world to see her genius. And I do. But not with him.

"Can I come home when I want?"

"Yes, you will have vacations," Augustine says. "We will always take care of you... Besides your family will know where you are... always."

But I will miss her so much, like cutting the boat from the harbor and letting it stray out to sea.

Angelica nods her head, "Yes." He is a liar, a swindler, a cheat, but she signs a paper that says she is his.

"What about your mother?" Augustine says. "Should I meet her?" At least he asks.

"I have no mother, but my grandmother will not like you." Like all her words, Angelica speaks these without pretension. "It's better that Carlos tells her—she trusts him." The payo writes his name and address on a piece of paper and gives it to me. I cannot read well, so the words are like scratches on the page. He hands her the wad of bills. I cannot read, but counting money is another thing.

"I will be back tomorrow evening by carriage to take her to Sevilla with me. I will meet you here at eight," he says. "What was your name?"

"Carlos Peña, El Huérfano," I say. "I sing mournful songs."

"Mournful? But Carlos, they come to our place to be happy," Augustine says.

"I understand."

"They come for the dancers," his hand reaches for Angelica's chin. "The beautiful dancers."

He will pull the tree as far away as possible from the root. He will bring Angelica perfumes and dresses and a life that will make her never want to return to Cádiz. Some payos keep the gypsy families together, others don't. Some, like Augustine, know there is power in taking someone away from her own home. But he doesn't know Angelica. She wears soft shoes but has a strong head.

When Augustine leaves, she turns to me. "This may be my chance, Carlitos."

"I don't trust him."

"He's full of grease," she laughs. "In his hair, his face, his shoes. Everything full of grease."

She trusts her strength, however—and so do I. As we pack her bag, there is no word of the kiss near the sea or what is in her heart for me.

"I'm going to be rich," Angelica says handing eight hundred pesetas to her grandmother. Juana holds the money to her throat. It is a precious gift, one that is much needed, but Juana looks at Angelica with very sad eyes. "I will be poorer than ever now that you are leaving—stay and make a family here."

"I am not far away," Angelica says. "You will come to watch me dance—won't you? And I will send you money."

"You will be far away," Juana says. She knows that the

world Angelica will enter will take her from all of us. Luis begs her to stay and marry, but when she does not listen, he walks out the door and down the streets of Cádiz and will not even say goodbye. In the evening, Juana, the children and I walk Angelica to the café. Augustine waits for her.

There are miles between us already. I squeeze her hand and release the yearning of my palm, send her to Sevilla where Augustine's world awaits. I watch as the carriage wheels turn against the cobblestoned roads of Cádiz. The one good thing I have known in life is gone, completely gone.

A wail in a grown man's voice can almost sound like music. Hah, isn't that the gift? To make all our pain into music, isn't this truly man's gift to the world? What would happen if I could no longer sing? I would have to live with the tears of an orphan in silence. Sing it, sing it in the mouth of flamenco:

There are two cases before the court
One true, the other not
There is nothing left to do
But bow my head
And say black is white. The truth lost out
Because money spoke here.

Yes. Imagine a song near the riverbed when the sky is dark and there is no one around—or in a café with a roomful of smoke and the odor of wine while La Culebra rolls her shoulders, roses tucked into her black hair. The muse cries out in a chorus of sorrow, full of pain like the ache of a tooth but with all the depth of a million souls. Flamenco is the orphan's music. My music. So you will find me in the melodies of the world, in the treetops of every forest, the voice tangled in the tree limbs in the mountains or the grapevines of our valleys. Flamenco's muse goes wherever we go, wherever our exile takes us.

12.
THE LOCKET

Es mi novio relojero
Cada vez que viene a verme
Se la para el minutero.

My betrothed is a watchmaker
Whenever he comes to see me,
The minute hand stops.

I shiver when I see Piedro on the lunar table. He is a small man with thin arms and large intense eyes peering from a dark face. Pure gypsy. I sit back in the chair. Saint Michael and I sit in the Palace of the Muses where the caged birds sing and water cascades against the limestone walls. Saint Michael casts a glance, a cool one, at me, and then raises his hand towards the lunar table. "You may want to run away," he says, "but try to stay still. Your mind will want to distract you. Curb it." The words rush through my frightened mind. I thought he was a thief. I didn't mean to. I just couldn't stop. Words, words.

Piedro's lone guitar stands near the bed. His fingers ripple across the strings, caress the guitar's wooden torso.

"Piedro, you are early," Mercedes says, walking into the room. She is pregnant. He bends to kiss her and pulls a locket out of his pocket.

"What is it?" she asks, her face filled with delight. Mercedes takes it from him, but not without a struggle for he loves to tease her, and teasing always leads to love.

"Catch it! Take it from me, if you can!" She tries to grab it from him, but he runs around the room. She darts at him until he is out of breath, and he laughs, his eyes shining.

"It was Piedro's gift to the woman he loved, Mercedes." Saint Michael points to the screen, bringing his finger to his lip.

Piedro puts the locket on her, and then nibbles on her neck like it is an apple, chewing into the moist core. "There. Where it belongs." She cracks open the locket to the face of a ticking clock.

In these days, I am alone and vengeful after Angelica has left for Sevilla. The world has stolen too many good things from me. I sleep all day and night and do no work. Luis tells me, "Sadness is great for songs, but we cannot live on it. Get to work." Pain paralyzes me, but it means nothing to him. "I have treated you like a son, and I depend on you now," he says.

"What do you need my work for when you have Augustine's money?"

"It will barely last through winter. You know how many hungry mouths I have there waiting in the house. I have family.

There are clothes and blankets to buy," he says.

I do not listen. I disappear into the streets and alleys, wandering. When I should be working hard for him, I do little for the man who has loved me like a father. Then, we travel to Jérez to work the harvest. I am lazy there too, with this sorrowful heart. I spend my days beneath the shade of the trees instead of pulling grapes from the vines. One night, Luis sends me back to Cádiz alone with food and a pouch full of money. "The diligencia leaves soon." He tells me. "Bring the money back to my mother in Cádiz. You are more useful to me on the road. Do not come back if you are not willing to work." When he tells me this, I break into tears. He spits on the ground near my feet. He walks away, leaving me there.

I wander the hills, ashamed by my weakness. If I were a true man, I would have gone with Angelica and shown her the power of my music. But Augustine has money. I think of him feeding pesetas between her teeth with the ease of a man who has always known power. But what do I have? I am weak and stupid from a sad heart. In the hills where I walk are raw old stucco houses without windows, like boulders buried in the long grasses. I find a tree several yards from one of the buildings and sink down against it as night falls. I take out my knife and let it rest in my palm. This way I can guard the small fortune and my bag of meat and cheese as I sleep. There are thieves in the hills. There are thieves everywhere.

In the quiet before dawn, I hear a noise. I can sense

things the others cannot—in the wind, in the voices of men, in the twigs of a breeze-swept tree. Any gypsy who has slept outside can distinguish the different animals by the depth of leaves crushed underfoot. Calculate the cadence, the amount of thought in each hoof, claw and step. No footstep is like a human's. If you listen closely, you can hear the sound of a man's thoughts in the way he walks. The pause, the calculation, the appraisal. The next step. Mind and footstep are so closely linked that with practice all one needs to do is listen closely to the sound of walking, and you can hear thoughts. The steps are headed for me, and I listen for danger in them. They pause as they reach me. I hear the steps of a hungry man, one who will take what I have and leave me with nothing. I leap up, my hand pressed into the handle of my knife. I can see him, but only barely, at first, as it is a dark moon. He sees me and runs. I chase after him.

With a furious leap, I am on him and drag him where he cannot be seen. I push him onto the ground with fury for all that has ever been taken from me without cause. When I jump onto him, I jump into death, like a free fall—*jump, Carlos, jump.* Jump into your rage, into a lifetime of persecution. My avenging hand points the knife towards his flesh, points to a lifetime of pain. A cry escapes from his dwindling breath, "Mercedes!"

"Thief!" I yell.

He is dark like me, but his wrists are fragile, like little

bird legs. He has thin lips and a broken front tooth. His body is frail like a twig. Just bone. Just bone. I do not let myself see a person there, but a collection of betrayals, of wrongs I have known, of targets floating in his skin. I aim for them, my knife in my hand. He struggles to grab at my blade. "Mad man!" he tries wrestling me into the earth.

But my knife's glittering goodness hangs over his throat, reflecting the silver dangers of night. The knife rotates in the air; my arms lose themselves and fly into it. Welcome home, Carlos Peña.

The stranger fights against me, and screams.

He is smaller than I am, and I have the power of death. I turn him onto his back and dig into the heart. Then I get off him and onto my knees, my hands on his mouth. I see life released—all that is sick and dark of life. Another time in the chest. I am kneeling beside him, to feel the expanse of surrender, little gasps of air, searching. The eyes let go and move into the constellations, eyes as round as Jupiter, pushed in orbit. I see life leave, so I throw myself again into death, as if in prayer, so full of blood and stab at him from neck to belly. Now he is just a thing, a bloody thing, that takes the rage of my days. He is not real, not a person to me, barely a face, but a slashed body, sacrificed for the evils that others have done. There is the smell of death, of birth, of released bloods. But he will never come back. His lonely head glares at me in the coming light of morning. It looks as stupid and lost as a fish on land laid out beneath a tree. I look again at his face, with a gash beneath the left eye. I grab my money and run.

In the hills near Jérez, the earth begins to breathe, Carlos Peña, Carlos Peña, what have you done? My fingernails are full of blood, cold. I have a dead man's juice on me. A dead man. The ground seems to move with the tremor of my fear, Carlos Peña, Carlos Peña.

In the house, St. Michael shows me on the lunar table, Mercedes imagines Piedro's face in the glow of the locket. Piedro has disappeared to find her something to eat, but she has waited too long. The sun is almost rising. She crawls out of bed and stumbles out the door to look for him. She calls his name as she walks out into the drying grasses, then pauses in horror. Mercedes falls to her knees beside the bloodied body. She screams with a terror that shakes the earth, then collapses onto her husband's corpse.

Days later, she travels to the gypsy ghetto in Sevilla where her mother lives. She wears the locket, tucked beneath her rumpled dress. She will never take it off. She rides the brown hills by rented horse, feeling heavy with grief and baby. "Piedro was murdered," she cries into her mother's dress. But he still lives in her. He lives in the weeping eyes of the baby girl, Altea, who is born from their love, two months later.

I fall back into my chair. My brow pulses. There is a throbbing there. I cover my face with my hands.

"I did so much... harm," I say. Saint Michael stands up

and shakes his head.

"How will you make up for this? Have you thought about it?" As he rises, the shadow of his body enlarges on the wall and ceiling.

My throat chokes back the words. "I don't know, Saint Michael." One hundred years have passed since Piedro's death. I look at the cheeks resting in his blood, her hands near his face. She loved him as I was never loved.

"Put your hand on your heart, and look into her eyes." I look at her face in the lunar table as it rests in the cradle of her lover's body.

"How can I ever make up for it? For what I have done? " I ask.

"Can you give her an offering, a real offering for her?"

"Like what?"

"The baby, kicking inside of her. Don't you owe her the debt of your heart?"

"Yes," I am confused.

Saint Michael walks behind me. He puts his hands on my shoulder and squeezes firmly. "That baby is now the young woman, the magician, Jeannie. Her soul has returned."

"Jeannie?" I turn around to look at him.

"Yes," Saint Michael says. "Jeannie was once Altea, Piedro's daughter. You owe her life, at least. At least that."

"And that's why I could not kill her."

"Exactly."

"Everything's so connected." I touch the place in my heart that says, "They deserved every bit of it," and I put my hand there, where the cool words hide the grief of the orphaned boy. The boy without a mother. That Altea. We are twins. I brought her what was brought to me. The same unfair fate, the life of an orphan. Jeannie, you are Altea. Now I understand. You were Piedro's daughter.

"But we are not done," Saint Michael says firmly. "The story does not end here, does it?"

My mouth dries with his words. I am afraid of what I will find out now, for I have forgotten so much.

I wonder how it could have been. The man on the screen, that Carlos, is split into two: the one who committed murder; the other who goes on as if nothing has happened.

This murdering self emerges, with blood on his hands, who cannot stop, who finds a beautiful abandon in the horrible act. I wash my hands in the river. I think again of that face... who was he? A gypsy like me? As the sun rises, I am gripped by horror. My shirt is soaked with blood, the blood of the man who has no name. The red stain sinks into my skin and bones. He and I will never be separate again. Our blood has merged. I try to scrub the red away, scrub until it looks merely like the faint shadow of dirt. But it will always be on me, no matter what I do.

I am frightened. No gypsy will report a crime to the police. Instead justice is taken into the hands of the people. It will start as gossip: "I heard a dead body has been found . . . ." and then revenge --and it is always brutal--is planned. Gypsy justice is simple and painful. A terror claws at my throat. My shirt, unbuttoned, slowly dries in the air of the coming morning. I run and I run with no destination, towards the north, away from Cádiz. As I run, it becomes clear: I must go to Sevilla—Sevilla with its large boulevards and new cafés. I could become almost invisible there, not like Cádiz where I am known. Sevilla where La Culebra dances. Where my Angelica is.

I meet with a diligencia later that day and travel to Sevilla. It is still hot, but the autumn breezes cool the night. I cannot sleep at all. I see Piedro's face again and again. I am haunted by the question: Who was he? Then I hear the chattering of girls' voices. I hear a woman wailing, she is saying, "That was my son. You took away my son." There is no rest for Carlos Peña.

When I arrive in Sevilla, my whole being is loose, undone, as if every seam of me is tearing. I want to find Angelica. She will be the healing hand that pieces me together again. I am falling apart, slipping into a slow kind of madness where there is no core, no center to me. The throat of a song, is all there is, an enflamed throat, a wound that seeks air.

I begin to search the cafés for Angelica. For days, I do not know how many, I prowl the streets. I am drunk all the time and spend Luis's money. I wander the streets of Sevilla and sleep in churches, parks, in the alleyways behind stores. During the day, I drink in cafés, losing myself in the blood of grapes, the tart red wine of Spain. At night, I watch the singers and dancers and will sometimes sing when dawn comes. There is a great madness in my voice, and some stay to listen, for this is something that rarely is heard, the sound of a man who has just delivered death, who has felt his own hand descend into the agony of its dark power. Most people fear me. I am dirty, my hair is matted, and my clothes are stained and torn.

Then she walks in. It is evening, and I am at the back table of Café de la Flor nursing wine and olives. Augustine strides in beside her. Her arm is in his. I am sure she sees me, but there is an emptiness in her face as if I do not exist.

Angelica wears a yellow hat and a bountiful dress with layers of petticoat and fabric, and her hair is braided in ribbon. This is no longer just a gypsy girl. La Culebra is something larger now, and she stares at me. She does not know who shames her more: Augustine, now that she is his, as she hangs on him, like his dark ornament—or me, her brother, her past, with all the worst qualities of a gypsy: drunk, red-eyed, dirty around the collar, smelling of the hills. She leans over and whispers to Augustine, then pulls him out the door. She tries to leave me there, but I won't let her. Drunk, stumbling, I follow her out.

"Walking away from your own brother?" I ask her.

"Carlos," she says with false surprise. "I didn't recognize

you."

Augustine reaches his hand to me, "Carlos."

"Yes," I say, "Singer of sad songs."

I catch sight of the face I knew, of Angelica, with her plump lips, and black curls now peering from beneath the yellow hat. I cannot believe that this is the gypsy girl who brought me to the ocean sand for the first time, who danced tirelessly and soulfully to my long laments. How could life change us in these few months? How could this white man, empty of duende, steal her from me?

"Dancing?" I ask.

"She is a sensation," Augustine answers for her. Angelica's silence makes me suspicious.

"Your sister is the best dancer in Sevilla. Come tonight to my café. You will see," Augustine adds.

Angelica loosens her arm from his and comes to my side. She looks at me carefully, beyond the unkempt face and crinkled shirt, to my soul, to the pain in me. It as if she remembers our love and in remembering, feels she cannot just leave me here. She also is of two selves. And I can see them. She steps towards Augustine and then back towards me. She is the wild dancing gypsy, and she is also the lady in the yellow dress with her Spanish patron.

"You look so tired. Why don't you come home with us and sleep?" She casts an anxious glance at Augustine, hoping for his approval. His back stiffens, and I accept.

"We have rooms for all our dancers, and I live upstairs, complete with practice area." His mouth forces itself into a smile. "We are family, and Angelica is the center of everything."

"You can sleep in Federico's room. He's away this week," she says. "Isn't that so, Augustine?"

"Yes," he says curtly. "You can sleep there. We're just a few blocks away."

The streets are wide in Sevilla, and where Augustine lives, they are filled with trees and jasmine vines. An iron gate opens to his large estate. I follow the two of them, still stumbling, and for moments at a time, I forget why I am there, even forget her name as I look at her, forget who she is, who we are. He opens the door, and I am led to my room by candlelight.

"Here," Angelica says. "Sleep here." I have never seen such high ceilings, and not a cracked window or a wall without paint. I must look like an old man, with my aching body and weathered face.

"What happened, Carlos?" she asks.

"Time." I look into the large room, then stare back at her.

"It's only been since summer," she says putting her hand on my chin. Upstairs Augustine's boots pace up and down upon the floor. Angelica's palm rests on my face. Her touch is like water. I am the thirsty earth that has found its well.

"Is he treating you okay?" I ask.

"In most ways," she says. "He wants to marry me."

"What a bastard," I slam the door on her and then falling into the warm bosom of the bed, into a dream that has no end, into the arms of a woman who has no eyes, and her brother who has no head, who keeps whistling and banging the wall, who keeps whistling and kicking the floor. A bird with a gun flies in, a bird with a gun in its mouth shoots him.

I have slept for almost two days.

I wake up a new man. A man who now forgets all he has been. Forgets the horrible stink. Forgets the widow's cry. Forgets the damning crime. It is the crusting of a scab, how the mind is, just like a wound that the body can forget. Knitting itself over the open red sore, new skin, new skin. I am no longer two men, but one again, the silver knife cleaned of its terrible truth.

I am El Huérfano, the cantaor again, Angelica's brother.

Above I hear the tapping of feet and the rhythm of guitar and palmas. I squint in the bright light and rise from the large white comforter. This is luxury. This is why Angelica is here. I feel pitifully poor; I have nothing to give her, but I have come to find her. I go to the basin, turn the tap and dip my hands into the running water to wash my face. In the mirror, staring back are stubble-filled cheeks and two bloodshot eyes. The person there scares me. The eyes are empty. I bring the soap to my face, scrubbing with strength, wiping away any hints of my sin.

I open the door quietly and walk the flight of stairs to a sunlit room lined in mirrors. As I look in, I see her. Angelica wears a dress of black with white spots and a red fringed scarf. She is as Spanish as she is gypsy. The girls on either side of her are tall and leaner, but she is La Culebra, the green-eyed snake, whose circling hips can drag the world into them; she moves as she always has with intensity and desire, toes and hands, and the belly between, as much fire as she is ice. She looks at me and then turns away, turns into the music.

Augustine stands near the window. His mouth is closed in a grimace. I cannot understand how she could ever give herself to him in any way, but I can understand the lure of the money, the scent of gold, the kitchen full of café, rolls and fresh fruit. What he has—not who he is—is appealing. How could she love him... really?

I turn to follow the sound of voices down the hall to the kitchen. I pause at the door because I see Lauro, Angelica's brother, sitting next to a beautiful young dancer.

"Well, look who's here," Lauro says. "Come to see the new gypsy music?"

"No. Not really."

"Our sister is quite the talk," he says. "Our Angelica. Everyone loves her."

"So I have heard." I step over to the stove, looking for coffee.

"You still singing?"

"I always sing. I sing when I am dreaming." I sit down with a warm cup of coffee, dark as chocolate.

"Carlos, this is Gema, one of our dancers." Lauro motions to the woman at his side. She has two braids wrapped around her head and a long throat on a short body. She stares at me suspiciously.

"Carlos is like a brother," Lauro says without emotion.

"Nice to meet you," I say, putting my lips to the edge of the cup. I've never tasted coffee like this before. It's good seduction.

"We're waiting for Piedro—the guitarist I told you about this summer. He'll change everything you think about guitar," Lauro says.

"I doubt it." I reach for bread.

"Really," Gema says. "I've never heard such good music."

"Good for him," I say between bites.

Lauro pushes the bread at me. "Carlos, you're thin as sticks. Luis been working you too hard?"

I drop my gaze to the polished floor. The money Luis gave me is almost gone from days of drinking, blind drinking. I will not last here long. I could soon be found out.

"No, everything's fine," I say. The dark well of coffee is hot. I pause without speaking.

Augustine then comes in with Angelica trailing. I feel

thirsty when I see her. It's a thirst no coffee can quench.

"Piedro's still not here?" Augustine asks. "It's not like him. He's never missed anything."

Angelica pauses at the door, takes one look at me. I feel she can see through me to the core of blood, to the ravaged body.

"He'll get here," Lauro says. "It's a big night. He knows."

Lauro and Gema follow Augustine out the door and up the stairs. "I need you up there soon as possible," Augustine calls down to Angelica.

She sits next to me, but she does so with the caution of a stranger. It's as if she is scared of me, and maybe I am scared of her, scared of what she might see.

"You look better now," she says. "What happened to you?"

"I'm okay. You happy here?" I ask. In just months, her eyes have become even more like emeralds. Her hair is well tamed pulled behind her ears, with sprigs of curls softening her face.

"Yes," she says. "Augustine's been good to me. I'm his favorite."

"Oh? His favorite what?" I tug at more bread.

"Dancer," she lets out a sigh. She clears her throat. "You got the money, right?" she asks.

"What money?"

"Augustine said he would send it through the bank... several packets of money for the family—and a small bundle just for you."

"No, I never got money."

"I'm sure he sent it," she says. "Maybe father never gave you..."

I think of Luis, and I think of Augustine. Luis is an honest man. There was never any money sent to us. Augustine lied. I know it. The man is a crook.

"He takes it out of my pay—money to go to my family. He says he sends it right away." Angelica speaks to me as if I am stupid.

"Sure he does," I say. "No wonder he loves the gypsy girls. They are loyal to their families. He's a thief, Angelica."

"Carlos... you don't understand." Angelica shakes her head.

"He keeps the money for himself. Can't you see that?" I shout.

Angelica walks away from me, up the spine of stairs, back to Augustine. I eat bread, more bread. Who knows when I will eat again?

Saint Michael darkens the screen, and looks at me. "What a sad sight you became." I look at myself, the image frozen on the screen. I am thin. My mouth is drawn in bitterness.

"The little I had in life was taken from me," I protest.

"You gave it away," says Saint Michael.

"Augustine was an ass." I stand from my chair and rest my hands on my hips.

"You did not even know him."

"He was stealing money from Angelica," I say.

"It's true." Saint Michael clears his throat. "And you could have been a hero to her, but instead..."

"Instead..."

The lunar table brightens.

While they are practicing, I sneak into Augustine's room. It is filled with the best wooden furniture and a large glass chandelier. A tall bureau rests against one wall. I look through its drawers until I find bills and more bills. It is packed with money. I take some for myself and stuff it into my pockets. Just as I close the drawer, Augustine walks in.

"What are you doing here?" he says.

"I am looking for the money you stole from my sister."

"What the hell are you talking about?"

"Yes, money you were supposed to send to our family. What did you do with it?"

"I did what I said I would. I sent it through the bank."

"No, you didn't," I pull out the drawer and dump the money out. "Who does this belong to... which girls?"

"It's my money—now get the hell out of my room."

"No," I leap at his neck, reaching to strangle him. He pulls me down with him. When he yells, the others come running in. The door flies open. Angelica and Lauro rush in. They see the money scattered on the floor--and Augustine's furious face as my hands are aimed at his throat in anger.

"What is going on?" Lauro asks.

"Get him out," Augustine says, standing. "Get the police."

"No, Augustine," Angelica pleads. She knows like I do that most gypsies never leave jail. It's a certain death there.

"Okay... then get the son of a bitch out of here."

Angelica looks at me with regret. I know. No one could love me now.

Lauro pats me on the back. "Take care, huérfano..."

I am crumpled up and so thin, walking down the stairs. My body is twisted in a pain that only mortals know. I slam the big wooden door behind me. I walk down the stairs onto the jasmine-filled path leading to the wide boulevard, and look up at the window above. I can see Augustine's back leaning against the window, his eyes aimed at La Culebra. I will never see the girl again. I know it. I look at the vines and trees cloaking the large stucco estate. I imagine stalking the building, my knife seeking Augustine. But I am still a free man now. I must leave while there's time. Leave while I am just Angelica's sad brother, not the assassin. No, I must not be him now. Not the other one.

I head down the long streets until I find a cheap café. The smoky room has a low ceiling and it is hot with the last hints of a cooling summer. Señoras fan their faces as they sit beside their husbands. I drink down a half bottle of wine.

At a table next to mine are a group of Spanish men who eat cheese and olives, breaking crackers against the rim of plates. "They found him dead in the hills near Jérez," one man says, shaking his head.

I keep my face down, staring into the wine.

"Some brutal bastard knifed him. He was slashed, mutilated."

"Piedro?" another man asks.

"The gypsy who plays for Augustine."

The words send heat down my spine. Piedro? I have little breath, and I am scared of my own voice, of the truth of my terrible deed. How could this be true? What if Angelica finds out what I did? Oh my God. Oh God. I check my hands for blood, look down at my stained shirt. I do not lift my head. Will they see me? Recognize my guilt? I imagine a guitarist with rippling fingers, and then remember the meat of a man left dismembered on the hill. Of all men in the world, could it really have been him: the guitarist, Piedro? Angelica's good

God will punish me. He will take my voice. I will never sing again. I down the last drop of wine. How will I escape? I am not a man but a demon. It is all too late now. I have to leave. And there is only one place left.

Granada.

Yes, I will go and find my father and sisters in the caves

near the great Alhambra. I will start life again. The money I stole from Augustine will get me there and fill my body with food for two weeks, at least. I will find Patia. My real sister. The one who could never deny we are family, the one whose skin was made from the same threads as mine. Patia, who held me in her arms when I was born.

"But before we continue there," Saint Michael says, breaking the spell, "there's still Mercedes and her baby Altea. Look up, now. Altea and Angelica will share a destiny."

"A destiny?"

"Yes, yes." Saint Michael brings his hands to his heart. "It is all connected, Carlos, like a great poem."

Curious and confused, I look up at the lunar table to see Piedro's wife Mercedes. She sits in the corner of a cluttered Sevillian tenement. The arms, legs and breathing torsos of her family and their family are crowded around her as she sits in a chair whose back is cracked. Mercedes stiffens as she coughs and coughs again. She coughs through the night, hacking and wheezing as her infant rests in her arms. Altea cries for milk, reaching for her mother's breasts, reaching from the cocoon of rags, to the glittering locket.

13.

ALTEA

Estoy viviendo en el mundo
Con la esperanza perdia
No es menester que me entierran
Porque estoy enterrao en via.

I am living in this world
Devoid of hope;
There is no need to bury me
Because I am buried alive.

I see no doors leading out of the casket, but the girl says there is a small flap that opens into the tunnel, like the bridge between mother and child that ushers us into the world. She will sneak out through the flap and into a tube and crawl to a small oxygen-packed room a few yards away, escaping the sand as it descends upon the coffin. The audience will believe she survives tons of sand falling on her, but she will not be in the coffin. It will only be their imagined death, the corpse of their own bad dreams, twisting beneath the suffocating weight.

Through the small tunnel she will go on her belly,

guided by her hands to the sprung door that opens to the hidden room. I crawl through the narrow passage, recalling the sojourn into life as my mother's body closed in on me in death, how I was almost buried in in the very place where life is conceived.

"Okay, let's run through this—Buried Alive--," Jeannie looks like a child in her sweat pants and ponytail. "Bring up the casket, load me in. The crane drops me into the pit. The truck comes from backstage. My cue will be when the wheels stop. Wait about thirty seconds. I'll slip out the coffin panel through the tunnel into the room below, then re-emerge stage left through the pile of sand, over there. Since Mark's gone, we're short a person. Would have been better to have someone in the room waiting, just a safeguard, we'll get someone for the real thing. We'll have oxygen next rehearsal. For now, if I'm not up in 6 and a half minutes, come and get me. Now," she cries out, the truck approaches the pit. "Good. Okay—back it up again."

"When she's going to stop?" Greg whispers to Sandra, shaking his head. "This is insane."

"This is her life, Greg... and yours too now. Better get used to it."

"Go, go be with the girl," Saint Michael says.

I sit on the coffin as it sinks beneath the stage onto the wooden bed below. When the crane releases it, I hear the truck approach. Its heavy wheels roll on the stage floor. The sand drops.

Jeannie's head pushes out of the casket into the narrow tunnel. She is on her belly, wiggling and twisting her way to the small room. She reaches for the door. It is so stuffy and hot that even I feel surrounded in it.

Jeannie pulls at the door, but it sticks, making only a hairline crack into the oxygen filled room. She presses her nose and mouth into the small pocket of air—and takes one long breath. Her nails dig into the jammed hinges. She tugs at them, with increasingly quick jabs, but cannot pry the door open.

Jeannie rolls onto her back as she gasps, steadily, slowly for air. I breathe with her.

Jeannie, I whisper. Orphan, you are also the tiny Altea, Piedro's only daughter. We can start all over again, can't we, little Altea? Here. Now. This time. Altea, forgive me. My breath is her breath, woman and muse moving as one. She leans into my arms, my chest. She stares into my sunken face without knowing.

"Jeannie! Jeannie! Where the hell is she?" Greg rushes down the stairs to the stage entrance to the air filled room and pushes at the trap door. "I'll get this thing open for you. Hang in there, Jeannie."

Then her spirit begins to ascend from her body. It is something I have come to know well over my years as an Angel of Death. Her fingers, her wrists, her shoulders, her back, her legs and arms peel away from the mass of flesh and skin and blood below. Her body enters death.

Now I see! She was meant to die all along after all. This was, indeed, some trick, but one played on me, Carlos Peña. She looks at me with confusion in her eyes—and I watch her turn to look again at the earth below.

Greg struggles until the door finally cracks. Hands sweating, the poor boy tense with fear, he pulls Jeannie Price from the tunnel into the oxygen filled room.

"Call 911," he screams out to Sandra who has followed closely behind him. He gets on his knees. He presses his lips to the girl he has grown to love and starts breathing into her. He breathes into her with all the gusts of life, the gusts of love.

I have been taught to never rush those who are entering the portal, for at first most do not understand. Where am I? What is happening? But then as if on cue, her face eases into a gentle smile. She looks at the commotion below and realizes she no longer belongs to any of it. She is no longer one of the busy ants crawling through life, mindlessly, carrying crumbs from one place to another.

And then she sees me and our eyes connect. Here on the other side, minds meet minds, above the frenzied chasing life of the Earth below. Her eyes turn to mine in both sorrow and hope. She turns away form that dead body below, with a kind of nostalgia for the person that body once was, and she is only and completely spirit. I extend my hand to her, and lead her to the tunnel.

Her gaze travels to the radiant shower of light at the end

of the corridor as silhouettes gather there. Unlike the one below, the heavenly tunnel is enclosed and infinite; there is no space, and there is limitless space. "Is that my papa?" I hear her thoughts as her face glows with happiness. I See Rick Price step forward, as she and I are carried by the light to the crowd waiting for her. Jeannie is home! She is home!

Her vulnerable and curious eyes reach out to me: "Who are you ?"

An old gypsy, I tell her, an angel, an old friend.

And then her attention turns from me to the reunion of friends and family who are waiting to usher Jeannie Price into the other dimension. "Daddy!"

And then as suddenly as that, I hear the whisper of the Great Creator, "Go back, Jeannie Price. It is not time yet."

The image of a beautiful crying baby with all the sweet tenderness of new life nestled in her arms swirls around her. And she smiles and nods her head in knowing, with a farewell to her ancestors, as she spins down through the tunnel of our Divine right back to Earth. Thump. And I am sent twirling through the tunnel with her, and land next to her and Greg, whose lips are still connected to her lips in one steady breath as her inspiration returns.

"Oh my God!" he lifts his head "Jeannie!" Quickly, the pink returns to her face spreading to her lips and fingertips. The rose rush of blood starts at the mouth and moves out, like sunrise. "Jeannie."

"What happened?" she asks, her gaze changing, softening. "Where is he?"

"Who?" Greg asks.

"The gypsy. Where did he go?"

I am here, resting my head upon her breasts, feeling the beautiful sinking, collapsing, opening, building of lungs and life within her. I am here. I touch her face with the grief of my memory: Altea.

"What happened to me?"

We hear the sound of running feet. "The paramedics are here!" Sandra cries out.

"I don't need this," she looks at the paramedics. "I'm fine."

"We need to run a few tests on you. At the hospital."

Greg holds her hand as they place Jeannie on the gurney and take her back stage. They bring her to an open door, into the light and the cool breeze, where an ambulance awaits.

"I can't remember a thing," she says, "almost nothing. What went wrong?"

"The trap," Greg comes close to her, wiping her brow with his hand. "It got stuck."

"How strange. "

"You're okay. That's all that matters."

"Where are they taking me?" Jeannie watches the closing doors, the pointed edge of a plastic tube hanging near her.

"To the hospital," Greg sits beside her. "They will need to do tests on you to see if you are okay."

"I feel fine," she says. "Really..." Her eyes close, slipping into sleep. "Just fine..."

To see her is to see the possessed. We are nothing, really, but who we have been, souls surviving. Jeannie turns to me, her hands above her head—looking right at me with a wide, wild smile. And then I imagine she sees him, the dark narrow eyes, the skin warmed by sun and sherry.

Papa.

***

Baby Altea is wrapped close to her mother in a woolen shawl. Hungry and without money, her mother Mercedes seeks her husband's boss, Augustine. She walks from the tenement to Augustine's café. Mercedes pushes the café door open and sees the great Culebra, not yet dressed for dance, eating her dinner.

"No beggars." Augustine shoos her out with his hand.

Her voice is weak, "I am Piedro's wife."

"Piedro?" he says, his voice softening. "Come in then."

He pulls up a chair. "Sit with us."

Mercedes watches hungrily as Angelica eats from a bountiful plate of beef and rice.

"Get her some food," Angelica says. "The poor woman is starving."

A waiter brings a brimming plate to Mercedes. Without

a moment's pause, she pushes her fork into the mound of meat and tomatoes.

"How are you surviving?" Augustine asks her. "Now that Piedro is gone."

She swallows hurriedly. "I have no money, nothing." Although she is now thin, a hint of her full cheeks is still there. She looks almost like a child, her hair tied back in a bun. "We have nothing now that he's gone. I am living with my cousin who has no food, barely room for us."

Augustine reaches into his pocket. "For the memory of Piedro." He hands Mercedes a palm full of bills.

"Oh, she's beautiful," Angelica says, turning to the baby's fluttering fingers. "What's her name?"

"Would you like to hold her?" Mercedes reaches the bundle to Angelica.

I pace uncomfortably as I watch on the lunar screen— with the memory of what I had done—stealing this poor baby's father from her.

"Her name is Altea." Mercedes strokes the baby's face, dark-skinned with large chocolate eyes.

Angelica laughs as the baby throws her hands into the air. "A little dancer!"

The lunar table dims and I sit down again. Around us candles burn. I wonder where Angelica is now. Does Jeannie ever dream of her, remember the arms that held her close one day in a Spanish café?

"Do people remember their past lives?" I ask Saint Michael. "I don't think I ever did when I was on Earth. "

"Happens all the time, but often they do not know it. The past leaks into the present. People live blindly, driven by who they once were, by old passions, old pain. People are possessed by desires and fears they do not understand."

I nod my head. "But if she understood. . ."

It could be so simple, really. I think of the first time I saw Jeannie whistling in the car, and paused, seeing more than just another target of death there, knowing there was someone, something else in her face. She was American, but not American, with a memory of Spain in her shoulders, a memory of my own past life. My soul held the secret: I owed her the debt of life for having taken her father. I owed her at least that.

"I want to see Jeannie. I need to see her again," I say to Saint Michael.

"Good." The angel rises from his chair.

"Will you help me find her?"

"Yes."

He tosses the pink thread down the hall, and it flies through the long alley of candles, to the palace's doors that open up to the heavens.

"Go, go now. God bless you, Carlos Peña." Saint Michael points to the candlelit corridor and hugs me.

I am startled by his words. No one has blessed me before.

I follow the pink thread as I have many times now, holding my hands onto it as if I am climbing down through the skies. I look at the great Earth below me and the stars around my head. Oh beautiful Earth! The frail clouds pass me, and the world below is freshly painted in rain, dew blue beads.

Without the burden of bringing death, I follow the pink cord past Jeannie's neighborhood to a saloon in the center of town. I feel I can dance again in the shade of olive trees and pluck grapes from their vines or swim in the turquoise sea. I slip into a room blasting with music. Everyone dances. On stage are the musicians: singer, guitarists and instruments and players I have not known before. It is new music with the rhythms of my old flamenco. I find Jeannie sweating from the heat of dancing bodies and the throb of music. She stands alone, eyes closed, her hair hanging in damp strands, clothes wet from spring rain. I press my face into her and smell her.

The music moves her like blood. As we dance, I am just the Angel of Death, with no hint of my gypsy body, just a skeleton, no muscle, no tissue, no flesh. My bony hands are old as if they have grown out of the granite sides of Andalusia's mountains.

When they were true hands, they brought death.

The ghost of Piedro stomps in with his guitar. My eyes meet his, pleading his forgiveness, but Piedro's small dark face stares into me with grief. "One hundred years of this... Good-bye, Carlos Peña." He looks beyond the fabric of Jeannie's white skin to the soul of Altea. She blushes with the chestnut flush of a gypsy girl. He snaps his fingers in the air and strums his guitar. Then he clicks his tongue. "Adios, hija." With guitar slung over his back, Piedro turns around, sends a somber kiss to Jeannie, Altea.

Greg stands where Piedro once danced and whispers, "I was afraid I would never see you again."

Altea has the dark skin of her father and the frail frame. Her long body moves loosely and easily as her black hair freely whips the air. Without lover or child, Altea dances, like a lone wolf with primitive steps. She has a power that is almost too big for the floor, could almost scare love away. Jeannie has this dance in her too but is afraid to remember it in herself. To remember Altea is to know the loneliness of death, of birth without the one you love most. Dance, Altea!

Jeannie turns in the direction of his voice, opening her eyes, "I am here." But it is no longer Greg but the gypsy Piedro. He puts his palms in hers and pulls her close. They spin in a circle, like lovers rolling in the grassy hills of Jérez. They dance together with the memory of the seas of Gibraltar, the caves of Sacromonte, the narrow, cobbled paths of Cádiz, elbow in elbow, with all of Spain between them. Her eyes open and close, aware and unaware, with the true magic of dance. The drum of his heart and the hot coals of her gut move man and woman to the rhythm of song. Jeannie's hair twirls about her while Greg dances steadily across the floor. She circles around him, her eyes meeting his, lover to lover, carried by dancing breath.

A crowd gathers, clapping, surrounding the two of them. As each person watches, Jeannie's steps become wilder, her arms like snakes as they beckon Greg to her. This is gypsy dance with the jaleos, the cries, of strangers, the making of duende, the heat that is built of souls, singing souls. "Eso! That's it! Dance, girl!"

But those who call out to Jeannie only see her short brown hair and American trousers. They do not see that she is also Altea whose green hemline orbits around her. And the rhythm, el ritmo, will never be forgotten, nunca se olvidará. Flamenco will not die. They do not see the gypsy tocaor, the man once taken by my rage. Two men, one soul. Altea, spin! Jeannie, round and round! Two girls, one dancer, one dance!

Imagine you're a gypsy with no food in your gut. Starving. So dance. Imagine that the winds are so cold, your shoulders are numb, your wrists frozen against your body. So you sing to the moon begging for the sun. Imagine that your mother is dead, but you push through her bloodied thighs into the world anyway. Sing, sing to our fickle God.

She plants a large kiss on Greg's cheek. "Can I go home with you tonight?"

They walk step in step, fingers clasped in fingers, down the sidewalk to his car. She starts to hum, the melody I have sung to her, and I am surprised she remembers. *Tell me that you love me, that you believe in me, brown girl of my soul, tell me, tell me now.* She hums and hums as she leans back in the seat, the window open to the scent of damp concrete. She hums with the sad joy of a gypsy girl, of one who has seen everything destroyed but knows the soul survives.

"That was wonderful. Dancing is so free. It's been so long, Greg. It's like coming home."

"I know," he beams back. "You looked beautiful out there."

In Spain, Islam's girls danced in circles, sheer silk flying, beneath the high arches of the Alhambra under the watch of a white moon. You can hear their feet in the waltzes of young lovers now dancing on the path of the castle near the caves of Sacromonte. The castle gates once gave way to trespassing gypsy girls with their caravans of instruments.

Today the old arches still lead into more arches surrounded in doves and vines; in the courtyards, wind-stirred pools reflect the passing clouds, just as they did centuries before.

"I'm glad you're okay." Grege holds the wheel of the car tightly. "You're not going to try that trick again, are you—the buried alive one... right?"

"Wrong," She laughs, her eyes lit with passion. "I just want to do it more intensely now. Maybe with flamenco dancers in red and black—gorgeous girls in tall long dresses, holding roses in their teeth. Can't you see it?"

It's okay. You won't lose her this time, I promise. She's yours. You are hers.

"Don't be so afraid of death," she winks. "And I won't be afraid of... well... us..."

I look down at the flashing signs of America with the greased quickness of light, so fast. No American church or fortress has stood as long as those of Spain. Even the pulpits of America's holy rooms are filled with infant ghosts, built with the hollow glow of new neon.

I head back to heaven, following the coastline with its green and golden rolling hills. I turn my back to the Earth and drift to the welcoming arms of Saint Michael, to a place where there is no matter, no things at all, no crumbling buildings or brightly lit signs. In heaven, there are just stars and the imagination, where we angels live between lives, between objects of our desire.

Saint Michael awaits me on a bench near the Gates, his wings swaying in heaven's breezes. "Carlos, come sit. It's a beautiful view." He is eating grapes from a basket next to him.

From here, I can see past the stars to the Earth below.

"The Earth looks small from here, but the suffering can be huge." Saint Michael bends forward, and rests his palm on his chin.

I nod my head and sit down beside him. The words he speaks are true. From here, Earth looks like a child's small marble rolling through the stars, nothing more than a toy.

"Congratulations." He wraps his arms around me in a grand embrace.

"Congratulations?"

"The lovers. From here, it's just a matter of time." Saint Michael's face glows with pride. He breaks the embrace and pats me on the back.

"Time?" I am not sure what he is saying. Am I becoming a muse?

"Here, have an apple."

I sink my teeth into it. I savor the sweet crunch between my teeth. "Delicious. I haven't tasted real fruit in decades." I bite again with re-awakened senses, every cell in my mouth has life again. I chew quickly and with joy.

Saint Michael grabs another bunch of grapes and pulls each one off with his teeth, letting them roll onto his tongue. "Do you remember anything about your last visit to your father and your sister, Patia?"

"Patia?" I think of that dear girl wrapped around me when the blood of new life was still fresh behind my ears.

"Yes," Saint Michael says. "Patia was sent to help you but could do little for you. Yours was a tragic life. Your angels could do close to nothing. Even Angelica tried."

"What happened to Angelica?"

"Come." He picks up the basket of fruit and escorts me arm in arm down the tree-filled lane. I look at the tall hedges on either side of the path and the large sculptures of birds, lions and giraffes in marble and gold. These are things I barely noticed before, caught in my own suffering. Saint Michael opens the door to the Palace of the Muses, pats my shoulder as I walk the familiar steps to our two chairs. He dims the light as I settle in. Angelica's face fills the screen. "We can't end without this." Saint Michael settles into the chair. "Your dancer, your love, Angelica."

"I am trapped," Angelica tells Lauro one night before she dances. "Carlos was right. I'm Augustine's puppet. My grandmother died with shame in her heart because I married him. How could I have done it?"

"It was easy to be fooled." Lauro whispers, so Augustine can't hear.

The world Angelica lives in becomes smaller each day. The more money she makes, the more Augustine forbids her. It begins as cruel words. Then he brings home new dancers and seduces them with his wealth. One by one, slips them into his grip, until they cannot leave. Angelica was once his favorite, now she is just good money—and La Culebra, the soul of the snake has been lost. She is just beauty and beauty is shallow without spirit.

She wants to go home.

A week later, Angelica, exhausted and sad, sits in a carriage that has stopped at the home of her father. A small group gathers around her. She is a celebrity in Cádiz, for she has traveled to Sevilla and made money and a name. She is dressed in wool and cotton, not just one but two layers, full of wealth. A large scarf covers her neck and lips. There is a hum of whispers as she peels away the veil to reveal a bruised jaw.

"The bastard tried to keep me from leaving," she says angrily.

Luis pulls Angelica to him with a kiss. At first, there is a light in his eyes, for this is his eldest most cherished daughter gone almost five years, but then pain flashes through him, and he frowns.

"What's this?" he asks pointing. "Augustine's?"

At Angelica's side is a little girl, about four years old. The others look at the child—is it his? The rich man's, the payo's?

"No, daddy," Angelica says. "She's gypsy. An orphan. I am raising her."

"An orphan? But these bruises are his?" He points to her arm.

"Yes." Her face dims with the words. "He had no respect."

"A gypsy man would have treated you better," Luis says taking her bruised arms into his hands.

"I know, daddy. I know it all now, maybe too much. Did you at least get the money he sent for me?"

"Money? I got nothing from him or you, just a heavy heart." Luis walks into his home, she follows him up the crumbling stairs to the crowded two-floor stone tenement.

"You were suddenly gone—and nothing, Angelica. I got nothing."

"You never got the money?" All these bruises and no money for her father? What was the pain for?

"I was right." I turn to Saint Michael in the dark. "Augustine was a cheat."

"Of course you were right."

"But I didn't know how to tell her. She wouldn't listen," I say.

"She had her lessons too, Carlos." Saint Michael strokes his beard.

"I wish I had been there when she returned. It could have been different."

"Everything could have been different, Carlos, but you were a dead man."

"Who is the little girl? Augustine's?" I lean closer trying to see the face.

"No. Don't you recognize her?"

"Altea?" My heart tugs. "Is that Altea with Angelica? How?"

"Mercedes died soon after her visit to Augustine's café. Tuberculosis. Angelica and Augustine adopted the child."

"So Angelica was a mother to her?"

"Yes—and taught her daughter to dance, just as La Tejedora had taught her."

The orphan created of my knife stands silently at

Angelica's side, gazing up at her with troubled eyes. Carlos and Altea. Jeannie and the Angel of Death. We are both Angelica's orphans, loved by her, brought to her home when no one else would have us.

But I never see Angelica after the day I flee from Sevilla with Piedro's death still fresh on me, in me. I run from her, in shame, in grief. I take the diligencia to find my father and sister, Patia, across the many miles of Spain to Granada. I never hear of Altea or the stories of Angelica's days as a star in Sevilla. Instead, I travel the ample boulevards out of town, with little money, slumped over in grief, in search of the one last hope.

I leave Sevilla for the gypsy ghetto nestled in the hills above Granada, in the shadow of the great Alhambra, in Sacromonte. Ah, sacred mountain, home of my father.

14.

SACRED MOUNTAIN

Cuando yo me muera
Mira que te encargo:
Que con la jebra de to
Pelo negro
Me amarres las manos.

When I finally die
Please do this for me
Take a strand of your
Black hair
And bind my hands with it.

The diligencia stops at the Alhambra. My shoes are worn by my travels, from being washed in the river too many times and from walking upon the hot stones and grasses of the first hot days of fall.

"Where is Sacromonte?" I ask an old gypsy woman. She points to caves in the brown hillside. Smoke from their burning fires drift into the brisk air. Night is slowly descending. The first star glimmers above the castle's clay towers. I have known all my life that Granada was home to my father and sisters. Now that I am here, it is like a magic land with its windy stone streets, and this magnificent red fortress, the crescent moon rising above it. I walk the curving road. Below, I hear the trotting of horse's hooves and the whips of their owners. Gay voices rise from lovers strolling in the paved alley ways of Granada. In the protected canyons, Spaniards are warmed by woolens and the kiss of sherry. One world below. Another above.

Here where the gypsies live, the wind blows. The flames flicker with no end. Families are crouched into doorless caves. I stop and ask if anyone knows Eduardo Peña and his daughters.

"They do not live far." A man points down the unpaved, twisting road. "Mas allá, allá over there."

I am afraid and tired, drained of life but also with a hope.

He will not refuse me. How could a father deny his own son? I think for certain he will look like me, but even taller, with a dignified head on a muscular body, his feet planted in the ground, his head circled by sun. He will be what I could have been had he loved me. And when he sees me, he will know: We are made of the same flesh.

I travel down one path and then another, glancing into the caves of different families, and searching for the sight of Patia. I think of the girl I once knew with her thin neck, straight black hair, eyes with the depth of a dozen wells.

"Eduardo Peña? Over there." People point in many directions, but I cannot find them. I soon become dizzy with the entrails of road as it curves higher and higher above the city and into the depths of gypsy barrio.

Then I come to a large cave. I stand at the mouth of it. It is dark, except for one burning lantern inside. There is a small table with several crates around it. Shelves are built into the walls of stucco and mountain, shelves that hold the Virgin Mary, a cross and a row of plates. I hear feet crunching gravel off the side of the cave in the open air. There a fire burns and a woman bending over, kneels to tend to it. She is thin with long hair tucked beneath the wrap of her shawl. She looks up at me and smiles. I come and look closely at her.

"Patia?" I whisper. She rises from the ground and searches my face. Her kind eyes tell me everything.

"Who are you?" she asks, cocking her head to one side, reaching her hands out to mine. "You know me."

"Carlos, Carlos Peña, son of Rosa. I am your brother."

"Carlos?... Carlitos!" Her eyes light up, her mouth breaks into a generous smile. She wraps me in her shawl with a long embrace. I collapse into her, like a pilgrim seeking his Mecca. I have found her.

"Come, come inside. Are you cold?" she takes both my shaking hands into hers and her eyes fill with tears. Some things change with time; others remain the same.

"Have some," she says as she brings a pot of herbs and

water to the table and pours. "You will need this. It will calm you."

I have heard of the Sacromonte healers with their herbs that take away the aches of men and women and change wild horses to tame ones. Perhaps Patia is one of those gypsy healers.

"I came to see you and my father."

"All this way, Carlos?" She hands me a blanket and brings the lantern to the table to see every crease and pore of my tired face. "But you will need to turn back. Our father will not let you stay here."

"But I am his son."

Patia leans forward, as if to lean all of her heart into my misguided belief. "Return to the place from where you came, Carlos. There is no life for you here."

"But I am his son." My voice is loud. I stand, pulling the blanket around me.

"He doesn't believe you are."

"What?"

"You are not his son. Or that's what he believes. You are someone else's."

"But he's my father."

Patia looks into my eyes with deep wonder, as if she sees exotic birds flying in them. Then she looks down at my throat.

"You do look like him," she says. "Eduardo is all over you."

"Won't he see that? Won't he recognize that?"

"No, no. It's too many years, Carlos. His mind is made up. You died when Rosa died. He thinks you were fathered by a payo. Understand? Go back to your home, your own life."

"I just want to see him now... I have no life, Patia." I slump back down onto the crate.

"No life?" Patia pours more tea for me, and rubs her hand against mine in soothing circles. "Tell me what you mean... We have until morning. Papa comes back in the morning—and he will have nothing to do with you—""

"But..."

"And I will share my stories too. Then we can go on our way like this was one good dream, Carlos."

"Why?" My face is filled with sadness. "Why do I have to go?"

"Still singing?" she interrupts.

"Singing?"

"You sang in the cradle," she laughs.

"I did?" I push the crate to the wall and lean back.

"Yes, yes," she says. "But not me... I don't sing well. My gift is caring for others. I take care of Eduardo and his new family. Sara and Flavia have married. But no children for me." She puts her hands on my knee. "Father has been a widower to two wives. I've stayed with him through it all. That's my gift. I'm no singer. But..." she leans into my ear and whispers. "I know why you are here. I can tell fortunes."

"What?" I am not sure I believe her.

"You have a troubled heart because you killed a man."

Some gypsy women can tell fortunes and even the payos pay them to read their palms. I have also heard that there are women who say only good things to please their patrons and take their money and lie. But Patia knows something. I just listen and nod my head.

"Am I right?" she asks.

My throat stiffens. "Yes."

"When I prayed the other morning, I was told I would see you again, but with this terrible truth." She starts to sing,

While the others see moon beams, you
Will see the light of my teeth, chattering.

"And what about this?" she says. "What the leaves tell me?"

I tell her of Angelica and Augustine and my broken heart and how I traveled back in the dark to Cádiz but stayed to sleep in the hillside. How my hand twitched on my knife with the hate of all men, not just one. I tell her how murder possessed me. I could not be the same again now. And by the end of my story, I am weeping to her.

"It is the curse of your birth," she says. "You are not the first gypsy in these hills to murder. It happens all the time. We have been beaten and hated by others so long that this is all we know."

"It's not that simple though," I say.

Patia pulls the crate next to mine, then leans into the wall, closing her eyes. She tells me to sit at her feet with my back against her toes and shins. She rubs my head, and I burst into more tears, long, long tears as she rubs and rubs.

"Poor boy," she says. "You'll never escape Rosa."

"Rosa?"

"She put the death wish on you when she died like that! What a curse to leave a son as you bring him into the world!" Patia says.

She strokes the back of my head. "Cry some more Carlos. Open your heart and cry some more, Carlos Peña."

And I do. I cry and cry about the mother I never had and the sad sick way I came into the world. I cry about being raped by Lorenzo and losing all faith in God. I cry about the sad love I had for Angelica, who would never love me back. I cry about the poverty of my heart and the few crumbs of food I have left, and how sick my life is. I cry about that poor body destroyed by my knife, and the sound of a tocaor. What was the sound of Piedro's guitar? What was the sound of his guitar? I keep asking.

I turn to face her with swollen eyes.

"When we left you at the Home for the Poor, I worried for you." Patia strokes my arm. "Grandmother had been so cruel to you, and you were so silent. A silence that was scary.

You never said anything back to her or to Flavia and Sara for their cruel teasing. So silent, too silent and powerless."

"Why?" I ask. "Why is this my burden?" I wipe away the tears with my hands.

"God knows," she says. "Some of us are appointed to be sinners and others saints. I take care of people. I lost my husband three months ago. Took care of him as he died. He had a monkey. I let the monkey free in the hills. In the parks of Cádiz, they lived in the trees. Can you imagine monkeys in Spain? I heard they escaped once from a ship... live high in the branches. Ah, Joaquin and that monkey!"

I drink more tea, feeling the sting of tears. I have not seen Patia in years, and yet I know her—and she knows me better than anyone does. How is this possible? We sit together quietly. Just sit. Her long gray skirt falls between her legs, embroidered in one corner with flowers. Her gray shawl is wrapped around her. Patia's kind eyes are as old as the night— and as dark. Her long arms are thin, like beautiful roots aimed for the center of the Earth.

"I have always been drawn to take care of others. Like you when you were young. I couldn't bear to see how you were treated. Poor boy, you have been imprinted with the death wish... but you carry it for all of us, for we all have it—"

"What is it?" I ask.

"There are two ways to unite with God: through life and through death. Some of us have the longing to join God through life... and others through death. Death wish, that's all... that's where your longing is."

She is right. While she prays for me, putting her hand on my head, I recall the wild rage of knife, how it longed for something.

"I want to see Eduardo. I have to."

"You are stubborn, aren't you?"

I curl up into a pile of blankets. Patia sits for a long while near the lantern.

"It isn't fair, Carlos. People divide the world into evil and good. For me it was the opposite, no matter what I did, I was always thought to be good. It's not fair. We all have both within us. The urge of the knife is not far from my hands sometimes, just as I am sure you can love well."

She sings:

I climbed to the top of the wall and the wind said to me,
What is the use of sighing if there is no remedy?

"Do you want to eat?" she asks me.

"No, I am too tired." I start to fall into sleep, every muscle in my body tender with the sweet release of tears.

"Rest and then leave before morning, Carlos. Before he comes home."

Crowing cocks wake me. I sit up from the blankets and look at the woman sleeping there. Black hair twirls around her face as she dreams, her hands in prayer beneath her lips. Patia. I touch her cheek, then pull myself up from the floor. I push aside the wooden slab that seals the cave and look out at Sacromonte. Smoking campfires dot the hillside. Dogs run up and down the browning grasses, gray clouds cool the air. Babies cry, and their gypsy mothers coo at them, while below a city comes to life. I take in a cold deep breath as I wait for him. The father who left me. Eduardo.

He will not refuse me! How could a father, a real father, and son not be united? Their reunion must be as inevitable as river waters pouring into the sea. I wait and wait, my body shivering. And then down the road, I see a man with three young sons, and two goats. He is walking towards his burrowed home, high in the hills here. As he nears, I approach.

"Papa?!" I call out, and run toward him.

He lifts his head, startled to see whose voice comes at him, but he does not smile or even lift an eyebrow with emotion. He is smaller than I had imagined with a round belly and thin legs. But his shoulders are broad for a gypsy. His black hair is streaked in silver.

"Papa." I am out of breath. The cold air combs my lungs.

"What?" He keeps walking. His boys look up at me with the cruel gazes of children.

"I am your son. Carlos Peña," I say.

"You are no Peña." He scans my body, trying to place me. He walks briskly until he reaches Patia. Walks as if I'm not there.

"The son you left behind. Rosa's son," I call out. Eduardo warms his hand over the fire while his boys tie the goats to a nearby tree.

"Rosa?" He throws a stick onto the small flames. "Rosa is dead—understand?"

Patia comes to her father's side, the boys close to her. "Go now, Carlos," she says. "Now."

But I will not. I have come too far and I have suffered too much. "I am your son," I say again with a voice that has been caught in my throat for years.

His throat bulges with anger. "You are not mine. I know my children." When I do not move, he tosses a stone at my feet.

"I am," I insist, and I dodge the stone, so it tumbles behind me, down the rolling slope.

Eduardo looks up at my unmoving frame, and leaps, pinning me to the ground. My own father presses his elbow into my throat, so I cannot breathe. My eyes beg him for mercy. And then he pauses. The narrow ridge of his nose aimed at me. He must see himself in my frightened face because he stands up with a snort, pushing me onto the path that leads away from Sacromonte. "Go," he says.

They all watch as I stumble away down the road. "You left me, you son of a bitch," I cry out and then head alone towards the highest ridge. Eduardo and the three boys stare angrily at Carlos Peña, the shrinking figure climbing away on the hills. There is no hope then. No hope in Sacromonte. Patia rushes after me.

"Take this," she presses a kiss into my cheek and hands me a blanket. "Stay away from the mountains. Snow is coming. Go towards town, Granada."

I nod my head, silently swallowing tears, but I keep walking up the hill, away from Granada, past the ridges of the barrio, onward across the highest peaks overlooking the Alhambra. I know I will find death there, and I yearn for it. I walk the maze of road past the white caves above the magnificent castle with the city beneath it. I walk in a sad trance, words and scattered phrases floating in my head. Son of a bitch. I am your son. You are not. I am. Come, daddy. Come, come here. My hands reach for my neck where his weight pushed into me, reaching to soothe the grieving throat. There is no home for Carlos Peña. I walk upward, upward without a thought, morning and afternoon, starving for food, but not hungry to eat, feeling the grumble of my gut and not caring. "Death wish," Patia had said. Indeed.

Late in the afternoon, I curl into a ball and rest upon the snow-dusted grass of a small meadow. It is beautiful and quiet in the foothills. I recall the feel of Eduardo on my body, the press of his elbow, the eyebrows furrowed in rage. Tall trees darken in the coming twilight. There are clusters of granite boulders, spotted in moss. The river sings over the yellow and red rocks, carrying fresh cool water. I hear new melodies in them and wish someone were here with me to sing.

The hills become steeper, but I find trails through the pine trees.

Then as I seek out shelter in the mountain caves, I feel a drop. And then the sky becomes light. Although it is twilight, an eerie white fills the sky. I make a tent for myself, using the blanket, sticks and boulders. Snowflakes begin to fall. The snow keeps falling, so I wrap the blanket around me and start walking again, searching for a cave to rest.

My fingers are frozen into small fists, as they clutch the blanket, tightened by the thoughts of my worrying mind. I do not know where I am. The heavens fill with a frozen white ash that falls around me. There is no beginning or end to it, to the sky. The snow keeps falling, the trees, the plants, the boulders lose all color— just one coat: white. With each step, I slip deeper into fresh sleet. I am breathing, but barely breathing, for my back and neck and face have become frozen. I am whispering, I will be there soon, papa. Don't worry. I am wandering blindly with no place to go. So tired. But I keep walking and walking and I do not know for how long, but the snow falls, and I am surrounded in it.

I get down on my knees. I think I will build a house for papa and me. I think, This is a nice house with a stove and a warm room. We will live here. I am on my knees, picking up snow. I imagine that I am building a tall castle, like the

Alhambra, with ice walls. It will be an ice castle, I think, and you can stay with me, daddy. I have been waiting so long for you. And then my chin turns numb with cold. Everything about me is numb. There is almost no pain left, so I rest in the fresh cool bed, comforted by it.

I do not have to fight anymore. I just fall into the crystalline world of ice, into the stars drifting in air, into my swirling warm breath. A dancer looks at me from behind the trees. She is dressed in green with white polka dots and a red shawl with fringe. "Do you know Angelica? I ask. You must have danced with her." She is pointing to my mouth, which is covered now in ice. I cannot speak, but I whisper, in a voice that has no sounds. "Yo soy cantaor. I am a singer, and you?"

The dancer is dodging the snow and spinning beneath the tree. I am drifting backwards, backwards. Do you know her? I ask. Let me sing:

How could you think that in the waves
There are not thousands of pearls
When I saw you crying one afternoon
By the side of the sea?

Suddenly, my breath and the snowflakes are pearls, and the air around me becomes one great sea, and the face of the dancer disappears into the white foam of a great wave. I hear Saint Michael whisper, "Ride the wave home. Good-bye,

Carlos Peña." I take one last glance at his kind bronze face.

And I am nowhere, but in the dark, being pushed into a body. The soul that enters a woman gains the heaviness of boulders. It is no longer weightless, slowed down, heavy with Earth's gravity.

"Are you sure?" he asks. "Maybe we should take it slow. You said you didn't want to go too fast."

"It's different now," Jeannie whispers. "Everything is different now." She takes his hand as he leads her down the hall. "No more waiting." She kisses Greg's throat and follows him across the threshold into his bedroom.

She opens her mouth, with the hunger of love. He gathers her hair in his hands, pressing his lips to her throat. Her mouth opens in joy, her head falls back as she sighs. His kisses make a trail from her throat to the valley between her breasts.

White pearls of snow, drops falling down, but now they are of the body, and they are all around, and I am like that falling snow in the red tunnel of her. We are swimming together, this sun around me and cool snow, and I enter. Sperm. Egg. The snow becomes a blizzard of blood. White particles pass me as I swim in the sea of blue and white, the warm water of my mother. But it is not quite time. I rise from inside of her, to the mountains of her body, hovering above her no longer a Death Angel, simply the ghost of Carlos Peña. No more corpses dragged upon my weary shoulders. And I just wait. Any minute now. Below me the sweet sighs of a man and a woman.

Life begins in the cradle of the arms of lovers, rocking hips, the flared bones of pelvis, in the receiving lips of her, widening to him. Greg kisses her belly, her hips, down her leg to her curling toes. Saliva gathers in my mouth, just the memory of a small pool of desire, in my tongue.

White skin peels away from Greg, shedding with the slow force of the Earth's axis, and I see Piedro, his body splayed out and sliced into bloodied wounds. Piedro, I whisper. It's you.

"You are bringing me life," the words crawl from his throat. "You bring me life now, Carlos Peña."

Papa.

In a matter of days it will all be forgotten. I will be just a fetus floating, no more Carlos, simply the unnamed. Piedro will be only Greg, no memory of our shared gypsy fates.

I will be his child. He will rock me in his arms to lullabies. But in this moment, I am neither here nor there. I carry both worlds with me: the grassy hill, with his life pressed into the earth, Angelica and Spain, country of my songs and the deep warmth of Jeannie. With each breath I forget who I once was although Carlos Peña sleeps forever in the hills of the Sierra Nevada. I am no longer a memory. I am grass in spring and the riverbed in winter. I sing in the valleys. My voice wails in the black granite of the hills. If you listen, all the world sings with these voices, the voices of the dead, the voices of those being born. Can you hear?

Greg's hands grip Jeannie's back, and he moves into her again. I hang above their bed, half within them, half around, then—I am pulled into her, by the weight of my new beginning, by the joining of his sperm and her egg. Now! Now is the moment! Piedro. Altea. I take one more glance around the room, then I am tugged in, going, going into the cave of her skin. I cannot ascend anymore. It is all down. Down, down into the girl.

Sacromonte covered in the rain of winter; Carlos Peña buried beneath the snow of the Sierras. The frozen, shivering self, sinking into the depths of a new life. I sing one last time:

How could you think that in the waves
There are not thousands of pearls?

In months I will be born again after one hundred years of being an Angel of Death. I leave behind the life of Carlos Peña. Will I be boy or girl? I do not know. But I will carry this throat and the rhythms of a cantaor with me. I will be a poet, a singer, a dancer although I do not know what that will look like in a child of the twenty-first century. I will sleep in the arms of Piedro's daughter, Altea, the bailaor, dear dancer. This time I will bring life to Piedro, bring the tears and laughter of a baby who has forgotten—who is born again as if the world is completely, entirely new.

AFTERWORD

*...we are first concerned with what it means for us to find
ourselves in a narrative relationship with a figure from another
reality. It almost doesn't matter who comes or what the exalted
one says. What does matter is that we are entering into an
alliance with an inner figure as if he or she were a living
person; the consequences of our relationship may turn out
to be as profound as any we've had...*

--Deena Metzger, *Writing for Your Life*

It is three in the morning. The crowd pours out of the
amphitheater onto the misty streets of Southern Spain. With a
clank, the gate locks behind us, and the theatre dims. I stare at
the darkened stage where the songs of the great gypsy singer El
Terremoto still resound in the empty auditorium, and the
images of flamenco dancers twirl, like ghosts, in the black
night. When I turn towards the streets to catch a cab to the
hotel, the sidewalks are already empty. Where did everyone go?
The chattering voices have died away, and not one taxi
remains. I am lost, completely alone on a corner in Cádiz in the
middle of the night.

I walk in search of a telephone, frightened, miles from

my rented room. For a moment, I think I hear footsteps, but they are washed away into the sound of the sea. So I turn to Carlos Peña, the guide, the character, who brought me here. He is invisible, without skin, but has become a part of my life as alive to me as my husband and daughter. It is because of Carlos Peña that I travel miles alone and spend thousands of dollars on a journey into Andalusia to see flamenco and gypsies first-hand. It is for Carlos that I am standing in the damp night; for him, I listen to El Terremoto sing out. It is Carlos Peña who has turned my life into an obsession with flamenco.

"Okay, this is your town, Carlos. Take me to Calle Marques, back to the hotel."

He says, "Don't worry. I know these streets like the lines in my hands, the ones that can tell fortunes."

I can feel his presence near me as I have in the years I scribed *Cante Bardo*. I follow him in blind faith down the Cádiz streets. He tells me he will protect me, and there is no need to worry. I will get back safely.

"Walk like a blind man at the hands of God. Just follow where I take you. I will tell you when to turn left or right."

"Okay, Carlos." My footsteps travel across the silent avenues. A car or two passes, but I keep my head pointed forward, trusting his guidance. It takes time, but soon I recognize the intersections of roads, a familiar streetlight, and the arches that mark the boulevard only blocks from my hotel. I am delighted but not surprised. I have learned to trust Carlos

Peña.

When Carlos first comes to me, it is a summer morning as I scribble in my journal. As I write, I hear his voice, full of breath, like a wind that is pushed between teeth as it directs my hand. "I am Carlos Peña. I lived in Cádiz, the town I love, and I want you to tell my story." It is a man speaking, urgent, insistent. I have written stories before, but no character has come like this with the power and presence of a real person.

"Cádiz? Where's that?" I write.

"Spain. I was a gypsy, a singer of songs. Now I am an Angel of Death." My hand moves furiously to capture his words.

"An Angel of Death?" I ask him. He senses my fear and chuckles.

"Don't be afraid. I just want you to tell my story." It is a laugh that is both sinister and childlike. I come to know it well.

"Your story?"

"Yes, I am like tijeras, like scissors, that cut through people's life, shredding them apart."

He frightens me. I want no part of it. "You sound dangerous. I do not want you here if you are dangerous."

He says, "I was dangerous once, but now I seek redemption."

Redemption? He tells me how he died alone as he begged for forgiveness in the snow-filled Andalusian mountains. He tells me he wants to start again and break free from the past. He tells me that he needs to share his story, and only through that can he begin again. He asks if I will only listen, and he will speak, just let the words come through my hands, and he will do the work.

Although I have written for many years, I am not fully practiced at this. I am both afraid and intrigued, and I can feel his heart beat and even the presence of his sex, imposing, almost threatening.

"So, girl, will you?"

"Yes."

I write for an hour as his story begins, and the next day I write more. His story comes out little at a time, with anecdotes here and there about a gypsy growing up in the late 1800's whose life was tragic as he chose death over love. In weeks, the first draft comes out on napkins, torn grocery bags, lined paper, in fragmented clusters and disconnected storylines. One day, instead of writing, I decide to watch television.

Carlos says, "You are running from me. You do this, don't you? Run from your own soul. You remind me of the shallow people who would pay me for my songs but then abandoned me to my own death. You are like them," he says, "aren't you?"

"I'm tired, Carlos. I need to relax. I work all week, you know."

"Relax with that little black box?"

I sink into the couch, put my feet up, and then the

television explodes—right there and then. The tube completely shatters. I begin to shake.

When I call to my husband, he assures me, "The television is old. It was just a matter of time."

"I think it was my character," I say. "It was Carlos."

My husband rolls his eyes. "The television's old. I'll bring it to the shop."

Was it the television? Or was it Carlos? Who knows, but synchronicities like this appear more and more frequently in the days I write Carlos's story. When Carlos is in my life, I feel a magic so profound that I learn to respect his requests, and we find ways to reach compromises. Working with him is an act of devotion for which I expect nothing in return except his trust. As I earn it, I get the joy of his story, his words, his creative guidance. He tells me to cover the clocks in my house because I am too preoccupied with schedules. He says that creativity is timeless, and I am trapped by notions of ordinary time. He tells me to read all I can about flamenco and Spanish writer, Federico Garcia Lorca. Carlos introduces me to places I never knew existed, guiding my hand through maps and atlases, to small towns, valleys, and mountain ranges.

Carlos tells me about the life of gypsies and the spirit and changing face of flamenco in his day. Carlos taught me of a culture and a time and of a woman he loved and a man he murdered. Carlos tells me of his grandmother who was beaten and tried in front of a gypsy court for infidelity. He tells me he was born in Jerez from a family of singers. Detail after detail crafts a world that is uniquely his, and when I read to verify the facts, most of them check out. So when Carlos Peña asks me to go to Spain, I cannot refuse. I follow him to Spain.

Traveling alone for two weeks, I feel I have a friend and private guide in Carlos Peña, who brings to me to the towns of his short life. "Look at what they have done to my beautiful city!" Carlos cries as we stand on the beach in Cádiz looking down at the rows of ticky-tacky condominiums and red concession stands. I later follow him down the old narrow streets to a café with yellow shutters.

"This is where Angelica and I played music." Later I learn from a historian that, indeed, that very corner was the heart of the gypsy quarter where singers and dancers gathered decades ago.

Where do these recollections come from? Is Carlos a part of my mind? Maybe he is no more than a reservoir of images I have seen and read over the years about Spain and gypsies. Perhaps, he is the imagination at its most alive, breathing into me with the power of fantasy. Or maybe Carlos is a part of my psyche, an aspect of myself full of poetry and pain, who emerges though the metaphor of a singing gypsy. Or could Carlos Peña be an archetype, a part of the collective unconscious? Wrote Carl Jung, "Archetypes... are living psychic forces that demand to be taken seriously..." Or maybe he is the memory of who I once was.

Could it be I roamed the hills and plains of Spain one hundred years ago? Is his story actually mine? Or, is he a spirit who has come for some kind of redemption through the telling of *Cante Bardo*? I may never know, and the answer may be something I cannot even now imagine. But it does not matter. My task simply is to listen and to write.

One day Carlos and I are sitting in a park in Cádiz as children play among the fountains and jasmine. "I wanted to die in Cádiz, near the sea, but I died alone, in the mountains instead."

Carlos looks out as the children chase each other across grass. "If you ever can, will you buy me a place here, near this park, Lisa, where my soul can rest?"

"Yes, Carlos. I promise."

I catch myself as I speak aloud to him, turning towards the jasmine, where he towers above me, his head surrounded in the halo of mid-afternoon sun. Did anyone see me talking out loud to him—or should I say to myself? Embarrassed I pull my hand over my mouth. Carlos... who are you?

And yet, although there is no answer, I plan to keep this pledge. I hope someday I can buy him an apartment where my friends and family can gather in his honor. Whether he is real or not, does not matter much; the voice with which he speaks and sings is the voice of magic, and to heed it, is to live a life that is richer, wilder, more full of sprit.

In Carlos, the real merges with the imaginary, and the

past intersects the present. His words are as alive today in Georgia as they may have been in Cádiz in 1895. I will always be grateful to Carlos Peña and his story; he sings it out like one long lament, with the haunting beauty of flamenco. Without Carlos, I would have never known of such music, of the soul of Spain, of the song which cries out in my own heart to be heard.

Thank you, Carlos Peña.

Lisa Smartt
Athens, Georgia
August, 2018

Lisa Smartt is an educator and author. Since 2014, she has been researching people's final words with Dr. Raymond Moody through the Final Words Project (www.finalwordsproject.org). Her book *Words at the Threshold* shares the early findings of their research. While she was investigating final words and near-death experiences, Lisa was deeply inspired by revelations of those who were nearing or had crossed the threshold and returned to share their journeys. *Cante Bardo* emerges from the realms of research and imagination and through the voice of Carlos Peña.